T4-AEC-187

Photo by Gerry Goodstein

A scene from the Circle Repertory Theatre production of "A Body of Water." Set design

A BODY OF WATER

BY JENNA ZARK

DRAMATISTS
PLAY SERVICE
INC.

© Copyright, 1994, by Jenna Zark

WHITE DAYS
© Copyright, 1992, by Jenna Zark
as an unpublished dramatic composition

FOREIGN BODIES
© Copyright, 1990, by Jenna Zark
as an unpublished dramatic composition

CAUTION: Professionals and amateurs are hereby warned that A BODY OF WATER is subject to a royalty. It is fully protected under the copyright laws of the United States of America, and of all countries covered by the International Copyright Union (including the Dominion of Canada and the rest of the British Commonwealth), and of all countries covered by the Pan-American Copyright Convention and the Universal Copyright Convention, and of all countries with which the United States has reciprocal copyright relations. All rights, including professional, amateur, motion picture, recitation, lecturing, public reading, radio broadcasting, television, video or sound taping, all other forms of mechanical or electronic reproduction, such as information storage and retrieval systems and photocopying, and the rights of translation into foreign languages, are strictly reserved. Particular emphasis is laid upon the question of readings, permission for which must be secured from the author's agent in writing.

The stage performance rights in A BODY OF WATER (other than first class rights) are controlled exclusively by the DRAMATISTS PLAY SERVICE, INC., 440 Park Avenue South, New York, N.Y. 10016. No professional or non-professional performance of the play (excluding first class professional performance) may be given without obtaining in advance the written permission of the DRAMATISTS PLAY SERVICE, INC., and paying the requisite fee.

Inquiries concerning all other rights should be addressed to Peter Hagan, c/o Writers & Artists Agency, 19 West 44th Street, New York, N.Y. 10036.

SPECIAL NOTE

All groups receiving permission to produce A BODY OF WATER are required (1) to give credit to the author as sole and exclusive author of the play in all programs distributed in connection with performances of the play and in all instances in which the title of the play appears for purposes of advertising, publicizing or otherwise exploiting the play and/or a production thereof; the name of the author must appear on a separate line, in which no other name appears, immediately beneath the title and in size of type equal to 50% of the largest letter used for the title of the play. No person, firm or entity may receive credit larger or more prominent than that accorded the author, and (2) to give the following acknowledgments on the title page of all programs distributed in connection with performances of the plays:

Produced by the Circle Repertory Company,
New York City,
Tanya Berezin and Abigail Evans, Producers

SPECIAL NOTE ON SONGS AND RECORDINGS

For performance of such music mentioned in this play as are in copyright, the permission of the copyright owners must be obtained; or other music or recordings in the public domain substituted.

A BODY OF WATER was produced by Circle Repertory Company (Tanya Berezin, Artistic Director), in New York City, in February, 1994, where it contained the second and third parts of the trilogy. It was directed by Caroline Kava; the scene design was by Loy Arcenas; the costume design was by Thomas L. Keller; the lighting design was by Brian Aldous; the sound design was by Darron L. West and the production stage manager was Denise Yaney. The cast was as follows:

WHITE DAYS
SANDY..Jodi Thelen
EDDIE/DAVID ....Bruce MacVittie
DEVI ....Stephanie Roth
BETTY .... Maggie Burke

SHOOTING SOULS
DEVI ....Stephanie Roth
GERSON ....Bruce MacVittie
RABBI JOEL MESSINGER.................................. Don T. Maseng
DR. NATALIE CARROLL ....Nikki Rene
MALKA..Jodi Thelen
BETTY .... Maggie Burke

FOREIGN BODIES was produced by Chicago Dramatists Workshop (Russ Tutterow, Artistic Director) in Chicago, Illinois, in November, 1990. It was directed by Doug Finlayson; the scene design was by Tim H. Oien; the costume design was by Dawn DeWitt; the lighting design was by Jeff Pines; the sound design was by David Zerlin and the production stage manager was Julia Hernandez. The cast was as follows:

RISE .... Lisa Marie Schultz
VERA ....Jan Lucas
SANDY... Lavonne Byers
MAY .... Deborah Davis

FOREIGN BODIES was also part of Circle Repertory Company's Lab season in November, 1993.

TABLE OF CONTENTS

FOREIGN BODIES 9

WHITE DAYS 41

SHOOTING SOULS 77

CHARACTERS

Part One (FOREIGN BODIES)
RISE (pronounce REES) — Early 30s, a would-be member of the Sacred Burial Society
VERA — Early 50s, a veteran of the Sacred Burial Society
SANDY — 30, a hair stylist and Burial Society member
MAY — A memory of Rise's mother. Age spans early 20s to middle age.

Part Two (WHITE DAYS)
SANDY — 33 (same as Act One description)
EDDIE — 37, chef and married to Sandy
BETTY — 51, Sandy's mother and ex-owner of the salon
DEVI — 30, an observant Jew and attendant at the Mikveh (ritual bath)
DAVID — King of ancient Israel (to be played by actor playing Eddie)

Part Three (SHOOTING SOULS)
DEVI — 35 (same as Act Two description)
BETTY — 56 (same)
GERSHON — 37, married to Devi and holding down several jobs
DR. NATALIE CARROLL — 39, gynecologist, African-American
RABBI JOEL MESSINGER — 42, clergy for local Orthodox community
MALKA — 40, a reluctant "Rebbitzin" (Rabbi's wife)

SET, TIME AND PLACE

PART ONE (FOREIGN BODIES) takes place in a funeral home outside of Chicago, a hair salon, May's living room, and train station. Time is the present.

Set: Should be a unit set, with a center area surrounded by other playing areas.

The "corpse" should be symbolic rather than realistic. Fabric could be used to suggest the curves and bumps of a human form.

If the washing-table is built with a hinge, it can be turned upright for the ritual washing at the end.

PART TWO (WHITE DAYS) takes place two years later, inside a Mikveh (ritual bath), an Italian Restaurant, and a hair salon.

Set: Same as before with a scrim stretched across an area up center. Pools of light dancing across the scrim will give an impression of water.

When the actress playing Sandy steps into the ritual bath, the audience should be able to hear the water.

PART THREE (SHOOTING SOULS) takes place five years later, on the Jewish New Year, on and around a bridge where a ceremony called "Tashlich" is being performed. Other locations include the Rabbi's study and Devi and Gershon's bedroom.

As before, there are divided playing areas. Bridge section may be arched, and basins can be filled and set out on the floor in front of the bridge, to suggest the river below.

NOTE: The scenes which occur on the bridge take place in the present; all other scenes in Part Three are either flashbacks or dreams.

AUTHOR'S NOTE

A BODY OF WATER is a trilogy about a group of people involved in three Jewish rituals. The sections are:

"Foreign Bodies,"

"White Days,"

and

"Shooting Souls."

One character from each piece will become the central focus of the next. Therefore, Sandy, who appears in a small part in *Foreign Bodies*, becomes the lead character in *White Days*. Devi, who is a supporting character in *White Days*, has the central role in *Shooting Souls*.

The following are suggestions for double-casting. If these suggestions are used, **the trilogy can be done with a cast of seven.**

Actress playing VERA in *Foreign Bodies* can double as BETTY in *White Days*.

Actress playing RISE in *Foreign Bodies* can double as DEVI in *White Days* and *Shooting Souls*.

Actress playing SANDY can double as MALKA in *Shooting Souls*.

Actor playing EDDIE in *White Days* can double as GERSHON in *Shooting Souls*.

Each piece can also be performed separately, if desired, or in different combinations (for example, using only Parts Two and Three).

FOREIGN BODIES

(Part One)

CHARACTER DESCRIPTIONS

RISE. A lab technician, in her early thirties, who decides to join the Sacred Burial Society. She is shy, self-protective, and trying to come to terms with her mother's recent death. In some ways she is like a plant that has been dormant a long time and is beginning to sprout new leaves — a bit prickly and awkward, yet strong and determined too. She can be stubborn and willful; also dryly funny; a loyal, intense, and adventurous woman on the verge of changing her life.

MAY. A larger-than-life woman who is mostly seen through the filter of Rise's memories of her mom. Brassy, bold, sometimes coarse — with a sharp, sometimes sarcastic sense of humor. Yet there is another side to May as well; a romantic, deeply loving woman who is brave enough to originate the Sacred Burial Society in a small provincial town.

VERA. A religious woman who recognizes that in the past she has sometimes taken herself too seriously and now can look back at her life and laugh; a "do-gooder" who is not always good, but who nevertheless is committed to helping others because it makes her feel better about herself. After being initiated into the Sacred Burial Society through an unlikely connection with May, she becomes teacher and guide to Rise, and the audience as well.

SANDY. Rise's best friend and owner of a hair salon. Tough, funny, glamorous, with a playful sense of fashion and style. Joins the Sacred Burial Society because she has a deeper side as well which she is not allowed to express in her role at the beauty salon. Comfortable with herself, and just beginning a relationship that is only alluded to here, but will carry over into Part Two.

FOREIGN BODIES

Scene 1

The Rayburn Funeral Home, in Ridgefield, Illinois, a southern suburb of Chicago. Time is the present. The stage is dark but for a small lighted area center stage. A corpse, covered by a white sheet, is lying on a long, hinged wooden table. Near the corpse is an end table with a basin of water, dipping cup, washcloths, nail clippers and pamphlets on it. Three large pails of water are also nearby. Vera is standing at the head of the table, holding one of the pamphlets and praying softly in Hebrew. Rise enters, looking around nervously.

VERA. Ba-ruch Atah Ha-Oh-say Shalom Bim-roh-mahv L'ah-vah-dahv Ooh L'year-ay Sh'moh.
(Lights up D.R. on May, sitting in a hard-backed wooden chair. May can only be seen in silhouette. She wears a forties-style dress and a big picture hat. Rise watches her.)
MAY. I know, Rabbi, it's against the Law, and I know in your eyes it's worse than having an autopsy—but I've done this for a long time, and the truth is I don't think I want anyone to see me like that. I know it's against the Law. It's not that I want a Christian funeral — I just ... I don't believe, Rabbi, it's not something I believe in anymore. So, look, I'm ... I'm leaving the synagogue, and ... I've put it in my will that I'd — *(Vera looks up.)*
VERA. Oh! I didn't see you! *(Rise, startled, turns around abruptly and gasps.)* Excuse me. I'm Vera Stark. You must be —
RISE. Rise.
VERA. Hello, Rise. *(Vera extends her hand, and Rise takes it.)* Cold hands, warm heart. *(Rise smiles tensely. Vera keeps holding Rise's hand.)* This is your first time?

RISE. Right.
VERA. You're May's daughter, aren't you? *(Rise nods.)* Sandy told me you'd be coming tonight. I said, well, she's her mother's —
RISE. I'm — I'm really not ... *(She breaks off.)*
VERA. What? You're not what?
MAY. I'd like to be cremated. I've put it in my will.
RISE. Nothing, I don't — nothing.
VERA. I hope you don't mind if I — I never got a chance to say how sorry I was about your mom.
RISE. It's okay. Is Sandy— I thought she'd be here by now.
VERA. What?
RISE. *(Impatiently.)* I THOUGHT SHE'D BE HERE BY NOW.
VERA. Oh, Sandy? She may be late. She said to start without her if she's not here by nine. Is that all right?
RISE. Well —
VERA. Maybe I can start by telling you what we're going to be —
RISE. Mrs. — Mrs. Stark —
VERA. Vera, please.
RISE. Vera —
VERA. Are you all right?
RISE. *(Nodding.)* Mmm-hmm.
VERA. It's hard the first time, I know.
RISE. It's — *(Pause.)* it's fine.
VERA. Well first we wash the hands, three times, over here — *(She indicates the basin.)* and say the prayer of Rach-ah-mim, asking kindness for the body. Can you read Hebrew?
RISE. A little.
VERA. Can you read the prayers? *(Vera gives one of the pamphlets to Rise, who opens it.)*
RISE. I think so. *(Rise tries to pay attention to Vera, but is distracted by the silhouetted woman more and more.)*
MAY. Frankly, I don't think it matters what we do. We're all strangers anyway.
VERA. We'll say them in English too, if you want.
RISE. Oh — Okay.

14

VERA.   Did you know her?
RISE.   Who?
VERA.   *(Indicating corpse.)* Mrs. —
RISE.   *(Interrupting.)* No.
MAY.   I've drawn up papers with my lawyer, and if my wishes aren't followed, you'll get a lawsuit, I promise you. I know it's a terrible sin, but it's what I want to do. I didn't —
VERA.   You stand on the left, I'll stand on the right. We have to wash every part of the body, starting with the head. There can't be anything that might come between her and the water at the end, all right?
RISE.   Yes.
VERA.   The nails, the hair, any bandages —
MAY.   I don't want him to find me again, buried under some stone in the town he grew up in.
VERA.   — eyes, nose, mouth —
MAY.   I waited for him long enough.
VERA.   Any foreign matter —
RISE.   I — I don't — *(Lights fade on May. Rise starts backing away from the corpse.)*
VERA.   What?
RISE.   I can't do this — I'm sorry — I —
VERA.   But I thought you —
RISE.   Sandy —
VERA.   She's —
RISE.   Will be here soon — I —
VERA.   Wait, let's —
RISE.   I HAVE TO GO! I'm sorry! *(Rise runs out, nearly tripping over one of the pails. Vera shakes her head, and looks at the corpse. Lights up D.L. on Sandy, standing next to a barber's chair. Behind the chair is a small table holding various beauty supplies — a spray bottle, hair spray, etc. Sandy is fashionably dressed in an offbeat way, with long polished nails, wildly styled hair and make-up. She leans her arm on the chair and addresses the audience.)*
SANDY.   The first time I went in there I really spooked. I kept thinking I'd walk in and this corpse would get up and go "AAAAAAAGH!" *(She lunges forward at the audience, and then relaxes.)* But that never happened. *(Sandy calls over her shoulder*

to Rise.) So, d'you get scared or what? *(Rise enters, carrying her purse and sits in the barber's chair. Sandy sprays Rise's hair with the spray-bottle and begins styling it into a French braid.)*
RISE.   You were late enough, weren't you?
SANDY.   I tried to call but you'd already left. I thought Vera —
RISE.   She told me. And then she said you wanted us to start without you —
SANDY.   If I didn't come by NINE. I was there at quarter to.
RISE.   Yeah ... well. She seemed like she was in a big hurry.
SANDY.   Really? I'm sorry.
RISE.   Me too.
SANDY.   It's okay.
RISE.   No it's not.
SANDY.   So it's not, don't worry about it.
RISE.   Was it — was it all right?
SANDY.   What do you mean, all right?
RISE.   ALL RIGHT, was it all right?
SANDY.   It was fine. It was lovely, it was — *(Pause. Sandy laughs softly to herself.)*
RISE.   What? *(Pause.)* WHAT?
SANDY.   Nothing a few dozen Häagen Daz bars won't cure.
RISE.   Oh, great.
SANDY.   I'm kidding. Hey — *(Vera addresses the audience from her position U.)*
VERA.   We're always trying to pretend there's no such thing as death.
SANDY.   I'm really not supposed to talk about it anyway.
VERA.   We shoot the bodies full of fluid and try to make them look like some kind of wax figures in a museum.
RISE.   Oh, come on.
SANDY.   No, it's —
VERA.   But when I came here — they said we leave them alone. And — they are cold, not freezing, but colder than we are.
RISE.   Tell me!

VERA. Still, they feel more ... human, I think, without the embalming.
SANDY. Well you're really curious for someone who —
RISE. Sandy!
VERA. We wash them for two reasons: to purify the body ritually, and to become familiar, I think, with that part of life.
SANDY. You should do it, I can't tell you.
VERA. It's almost — it's very intimate, really. You wash down one side, and turn them over so they're facing you, gently —
RISE. You got me into this!
SANDY. YOU volunteered.
RISE. So did you.
VERA. And you say, "Please forgive us for any indignity we may commit, unknowingly ..."
SANDY. I had my own reasons, you had yours. Right? *(Pause.)* RIGHT?
VERA. And you hope there will be someone else who will be kind to you. *(Vera becomes still, looking at the corpse.)*
RISE. Right.
SANDY. Okay?
RISE. Okay.
SANDY. Damn! Wait a sec. *(She unravels part of the braid and starts again.)*
RISE. You know sometimes if you can see something first-hand it's, well. Anyway. *(Sighs.)* It was a bad idea.
SANDY. When my aunt died I wanted to learn how to deal with it.
RISE. So did it help?
SANDY. No. *(Rise smiles. Sandy finishes the braid.)* You ... want a bow?
RISE. *(Wrinkling her nose.)* No!
SANDY. I don't mean a big one, look! *(She takes a rawhide tie from her table and shows it to Rise.)*
RISE. *(Smiling.)* Oh great. Cowgirls on the Rio Grande.
SANDY. You wish. *(They laugh.)* Listen, when are you going to come see us? *(Rise gets up.)*
RISE. I don't know.

SANDY. You mad I moved out?
RISE. *(Emphatic.)* NO, I'm not mad you moved out! Will you stop asking me please?
SANDY. What, to come over, or if you're mad?
RISE. Either. Just don't worry about it okay? I understand.
SANDY. I know, but I think Eddie is —
RISE. Eddie's great, I'm just —
SANDY. I want you to come see us. Okay?
RISE. Okay, okay. You gonna marry this guy or what?
SANDY. I don't know. He has to prove himself in bed first.
RISE. *(Laughing.)* How much do I owe?
SANDY. Nothing.
RISE. Sandy!
SANDY. Next time. *(Rise reaches into her purse for some cash.)*
RISE. You're going to take money today. Five! At least take five! *(Rise hands Sandy the money and turns to leave. Sandy quickly puts the money inside Rise's shirt.)* Help! Stop that!
SANDY. Don't mess with me!
RISE. Don't mess with ME! *(Rise exits. Sandy walks over to Vera and the corpse. Sandy takes the basin from the table and holds it while Vera takes a dipping cup and fills it with water. She pours the water over each hand, refilling the cup and repeating this three times. Vera then holds the basin for Sandy, who washes her hands in the same manner. The women say the following.)*
VERA. Ree – Bone – Oh Shell Oh – Lum
SANDY. God of the Universe
VERA. Have compassion for Miriam, baht Shoshanna.
SANDY. Daughter of Shoshanna, this deceased, for she is a descendant of Abraham, Isaac and Jacob, Your servants.
VERA. May her soul and spirit rest with the righteous, for You are He who revives the dead and brings death to the living. *(Sandy turns to the audience.)*
SANDY. When I was in beauty school we had this crazy instructor Mr. Wafa-something, from Afghanistan, and his brother owned a funeral home down in Hammond. Anyway he used to make us practice on the corpses. Makeup and hair, I mean. Nails too if there was time. *(She fills the cup*

again.) He said — what did he say? *(Affecting a British accent.)* "Like a little gift you give them before they go. A bit of blush. A manicure." But you know, it's a real pain in the ass putting makeup on these guys, and we were students so we didn't get paid. They charged the customers plenty though — it's expensive if you want that shit, don't think it's not. Anyway, I'm really glad we don't do it here. Mine were always coming out green no matter how much base I used. *(Vera puts the basin down and lifts the top of the sheet off the corpse's head. Sandy pours the water over the head while Vera addresses the audience.)*

VERA.   Funny how you — I was sitting in shul one morning and our rabbi started asking the congregation for volunteers. He called it the "Hev-ra Ka-dee-sha" — Sacred Burial Society. And I thought, my God, how can anyone — How can he ask us that? Because when my father died, a couple came and took care of him. They were — I remember peeking at them in the kitchen. I had to go the bathroom but I was so scared — I couldn't go across. It was like that river, what do they call it? The Styx. *(Lights up D.R. on Rise, a towel draped around her shoulders, sitting on a bed, holding a phone to her ear. Her hair is slightly damp. A hairbrush is also on the bed. May, in silhouetted profile, sits U. of Rise.)*

RISE.   San? If you're there pick up. *(She taps her foot impatiently.)* I had another blow-out with my boss today. I keep telling him we're a hospital, not G.M., but —

VERA.   And then my mother came in and she took me to bed. But I never forgot them and when he — I was sitting there thinking about radishes, it was March, and I wanted to put the radishes in, and then I hear the rabbi talking about Abraham. Well that's nothing, rabbis are always saying something about Abraham. But then he started talking about Sarah's burial, and I thought, uh-oh, what's this?

RISE.   Anyway, I thought I'd call and see if you wanted to go out, but — It's funny, I keep thinking you're here, and uh — *(Her voice wavers.)* you're going to get mad at me because the hot water's gone off and you say —

MAY. *(Softly.)* Did you take a shower?
RISE. *(Confused.)* What?
VERA. What did he call it? A mitzvah — a good deed. The biggest one of all, in fact, because you couldn't be paid back. *(Laughs.)* Ha! My husband didn't think it was such a mitzvah — in fact what he said was —
MAY. DID YOU TAKE A SHOWER?
RISE. *(Shakily.)* Well ... bye. *(Rise hangs up, and sits, staring into space. Vera and Sandy pick up their pamphlets and pray, moving their lips silently. From time to time the praying gets louder, and is heard as an undercurrent to the following dialogue, sometimes even interrupting it, as shown.)*
MAY. I used to go on weekends to visit your father. I would have to leave after work on Friday and then I didn't get to Washington until 9 or 10. And Sunday night I'd come back. But in those days you couldn't get a train at seven or eight. They were all full of soldiers. So I'd have to take the ten-thirty-five out of Washington. And I'd get back to the city at one or two in the morning.
VERA. Y'hee Rah-tzone Mil-faw-neh-cha Elohay-nu
        V'ale-ohay Ah-voh-tay-nu —
MAY. It was too late to go home on the subway. My mother lived in Brooklyn and I was living with her while he was in the army. And the cabs were too high for me.
RISE. Huh?
MAY. I said the cabs were too high. By that I mean I couldn't pay.
SANDY. Ba-Ruch Atah Koh-Rayt Hah B'rit
        B'ra-cha-mim B'ra-cha-mim.
MAY. So I sat up on one of the benches in Grand Central.
RISE. All night?
MAY. And then about seven, I went to the ladies room and washed my face, and then I went to work. I wasn't the only one who sat up like that.
VERA. Baruch atah Ha – No Tane Ra-cha-mim Gid-oh-lim.
MAY. So — who died? *(Pause.)* Don't look at me like that. You went to the washing last night. Who died?

RISE. Mrs. Weiss.
MAY. Wein, you mean, don't you? Marilyn Wein?
RISE. I don't know.
MAY. She frightened you?
RISE. No. *(Rise picks up the brush and starts brushing out her hair.)*
MAY. Honey, you know they're going to call you again.
RISE. No they're not.
MAY. You mark my words, she'll call you tonight.
RISE. Just leave it alone, all right?
MAY. Fine, suit yourself. I don't know why you want to spend your time in a funeral home anyway.
RISE. You did.
MAY. That's different. I was married already.
RISE. What's that got to do with it?
MAY. Plenty. You spend your life with dead people you wind up dead.
RISE. I don't spend my life with — *(Pause, as she looks at May.)* I don't spend my WHOLE life with dead people.
MAY. What did you say? I can't hear you. Would you speak up please? *(Pause, as May smiles.)* I thought so.
RISE. I just —
MAY. Listen, Rise. You know the sweetest words a mother can hear from her daughter?
RISE. Don't tell me. Let me guess.
MAY. Life, ma. I'm feeling life.
RISE. What life?
MAY. In the belly. You know what I'm talking about? *(Sighs.)* Smart like two colleges, my daughter.
RISE. I'm sorry to disappoint you.
MAY. Sorry, you're not.
RISE. All right, I'm not.
MAY. I would've liked to see you under the canopy. Just once.
RISE. Only once? You're sure?
MAY. Don't be so fresh.
RISE. I'm not fresh.

MAY. What are you afraid of?
RISE. I'm not.
MAY. So why are you alone?
RISE. I'm not alone.
MAY. That's funny, you look pretty alone to me. *(Pause.)* What is it? What's going on with you?
RISE. Nothing.
MAY. Nothing. You know that was the first word you said? I remember you were a little bitty thing, leaning against the door one morning when I was drinking coffee, and I said, Rise, what are you doing? And you said, "Noth – ing." *(Pause. The praying has stopped. Sandy and Vera are still. Rise puts down the brush.)*
RISE. Mom —
MAY. Yes?
RISE. Remember the Wenders party? When I was ten?
MAY. The Wenders?
RISE. They lived next door and they had a big —
MAY. Oh, yes, when the son got married.
RISE. There was a couple sitting on the couch and the woman was sick?
MAY. What couple?
RISE. She had something wrong with her. A stroke or something.
MAY. That I don't remember.
RISE. And the other women were all clucking around and saying "poor thing" and stuff — *(Sandy and Vera interrupt, clicking their tongues and making soft, sympathetic sounds.)*
VERA. Poor thing.
SANDY. What a shame!
MAY. That's ridiculous.
RISE. I remember it.
MAY. You always imagined things.
RISE. She was shaking all over the place and he was holding her so she wouldn't fall.
MAY. You had imaginary friends.
RISE. It's true!

MAY.   So what if it's true, what does it have to do with you?
RISE.   She kept trying to talk but ... all she could do was move her mouth and make these sounds ... "mmmm — vawww" — she was trying so hard I almost felt like she was saying "Wait!"
SANDY.   Wait!
VERA.   Wait!
RISE.   "That's not me! I'm over here, see? The beautiful blonde in the black dress, by the window! Not this awful — not on the couch —"
SANDY.   Poor thing!
RISE.   I mean I used to feel that way when you'd come in my room —
MAY.   When?
RISE.   What do you mean, when? We never had any locks on our doors, remember? You came in whenever you felt like it. All the time.
MAY.   If I needed something, I —
RISE.   Whether you needed it or not, you'd come in. And I'd be there with this towel on my head and you'd say —
MAY.   What are you doing?
RISE.   And I'd be — you know — like the heroines in the movies about the underground. *(She wraps the towel around her head.)*
MAY.   Which underground?
RISE.   Like the French had during the war. And I'd have these big dark eyes and long hair to my knees, but I'd wear it up, in braids around my head and then ... with my lover I'd let it down at night. *(Slowly, she unwraps the towel and lets it fall around her shoulders.)* And he'd say —
MAY.   You washed your hair again?
RISE.   Yes. Yes I did.
MAY.   How many times is that?
RISE.   And then he'd be in trouble somehow — the townspeople would accuse him of being a collaborator —
MAY.   What's that smell?
RISE.   And I'd push through, I'd push through them and

stand in front of him and throw down my shawl. *(She throws the towel down on the floor.)* I don't know why but it seems like something they'd do in a movie like that.
MAY. You've been smoking in here, haven't you?
RISE. No, I'd say, it's not true! Whatever you think, it's not him. And I'd look around, and pick out the angriest face, and I'd find her in that mob of fury and all I could see in her eyes was —
MAY. What is the matter with you?
RISE. Rage, burning the air with her rage, and —
MAY. HEY!!
RISE. I'd see —
MAY. Rise! I'm talking to you!
RISE. I'd see you ... standing there, looking at me like I was crazy and you'd say —
MAY. WHAT are you DOING?
RISE. And all I could do was look at the floor and say, "nothing." Like that woman on the couch.
MAY. What woman?
RISE. She couldn't tell anyone who she was because she — wasn't. You know?
MAY. No. I don't know.
RISE. I mean there must have been a time when she was sexy, and beautiful, and — and he liked to look at her breasts — *(May groans.)* And then she had a stroke and the only thing he saw when he looked at her was —
VERA. Poor thing! *(Sandy and Vera cluck their tongues.)*
RISE. And then what were they left with? Mom?
MAY. Honey, it's not them I'm worried about, it's you.
RISE. I just want to know —
MAY. People are human, all right? They come in without knocking! They get sick, they die! It happens sometimes.
RISE. I don't want it to happen to me.
MAY. You don't want anything to happen to you.
RISE. Maybe I don't.
MAY. You're like a little old lady, you know? You get up, you go to work, you come home, you take a nap —

RISE. I'm tired —
MAY. You know what it is, when a woman cheats herself?
RISE. I'm not cheating myself!
MAY. When a man cheats you it's one thing. Even when a friend cheats you out of a man. But when a woman cheats herself it's shanda. You know what that means?
RISE. Please, ma —
MAY. You hear me? Shame, shame, shame! *(Lights fade on this scene.)*

Scene 2

Lights up on Vera up center. Sandy is downstage left, watching her.

VERA. By the time I met this woman I was in the throes of a — what do you call it — revival. I wasn't raised orthodox, but after I'd been married a few years I wanted to follow the Laws — keep kosher, light the candles Friday night, do mitzvahs — and Hev-ra Kah-dee-sha was part of that. Because it was something most people wouldn't do, and — I guess I always wanted to be, well, I liked doing things other people couldn't do. So, you have to understand, May was very offensive to me. She was what we call a twice-a-year Jew — she came to shul on Rosh Hashanah to say Happy New Year to her friends, and on Yom Kippur to beg a little forgiveness for another year. And here it is, the holiest day of the year and she's taking a break from services in the parking lot. *(Lights up on May U.L., smoking a cigarette. She wears a light topcoat, and no hat.)*
MAY. *(Startled.)* Oh. Hello. *(Vera shakes her head no, giving May a disapproving look.)* I just thought I'd take a little —
VERA. It's against the Law to smoke on a holiday.
MAY. What law?
VERA. The Torah. You know what a Torah is, don't you?
MAY. *(Snidely.)* On Yom Kippur they all get so good. *(May*

gives Vera a contemptuous look, crushing the cigarette under her heel.)
VERA. I think she held it against Ben — his wanting to come back here. She was hoping he'd find something in New York, where she was from. But his family had a restaurant and they asked him to help — you know how that goes. She didn't have much to say about Ridgefield.
MAY. Flat as a board game and stinks to high heaven. Like an old man in a paint factory breaking wind.
VERA. It was funny, though, Ben was the one who left in the end and she was the one who stayed. And all she would say when we asked where he'd gone was —
MAY. Parts unknown —
VERA. Parts unknown, and she had just that one daughter, Rise, her name was, and she went to work selling real estate. For someone who hated the neighborhood she did pretty well.
MAY. At twenty thousand it's a steal. You'll double the asking price in ten years.
VERA. The steel mills were booming. And she got herself a nice house, too. Though she still complained of the smell sometimes.
MAY. Like an old man's breath in the middle of the night.
VERA. So you can imagine how shocked I was — not just surprised, you know, I was really shocked — when I walked in to the room and of all people to see there — *(May approaches Vera from behind.)*
MAY. What are you doing here?
VERA. *(Gasps.)* Oh! You scared me!
MAY. You're doing this today?
VERA. I'm — Are YOU?
MAY. I was the one who started this out here. I thought you knew that.
VERA. My God.
MAY. *(Sarcastically.)* Mine too.
VERA. What? *(Pause.)* What did you say?
MAY. *(Smiles, to herself.)* Nothing much. You've, uh, done this before?

VERA. No.
MAY. Well. Is Sophie coming today, do you know?
VERA. She called and said she wasn't feeling well.
MAY. So I guess we're it, then, huh?
VERA. Looks that way.
MAY. You want to start, then?
VERA. Sure. *(Pause.)* You just — start washing, right?
MAY. First you do the head, and go down the right side, and then again on the left.
VERA. All right.
MAY. So, what are you waiting for, a train?
VERA. No. *(Vera turns, angrily, and picks up a washcloth. She dips it in a bucket of water and wrings it out. Then she turns back to the body but does not move. The women stare at each other for a moment. Then, slowly, almost sensuously, May reaches out and begins lifting the sheet off the corpse's head. Vera gasps, involuntarily.)* Oh!
MAY. You all right?
VERA. *(Stammering.)* Fine, I'm — fi — I —
MAY. You want to use the comb? *(May picks up a comb and hands it to Vera, who takes it but cannot bring herself to look at the body.)*
VERA. I'm fine, I'm fine.
MAY. You look fine.
VERA. I am.
MAY. You look swell.
VERA. I'm fine.
MAY. I see that. You want to do the hair?
VERA. Sure. *(Vera doesn't move. After a beat, May takes the comb and begins combing the body's hair gently.)*
MAY. Ah. She has a nice head of hair, doesn't she?
VERA. Yes ...
MAY. *(Reciting.)* "Her head is like the most fine gold; her heaps of curls are black as a raven."
VERA. What's that?
MAY. We say these prayers when we're washing them — you want to hold that book for me? *(May indicates the prayer book on the table with a nod of her head. Vera puts the cloth down,*

picks up the book and opens it. She holds it up, trembling, while May reads.) Page 3. *(Vera shakily turns the page.)* "Her eyes are like doves beside the water-brooks, bathing in milk and fitly set."
VERA.   May, I —
MAY.   Then we take the cloth, and very gently, wash the face. *(May picks up the cloth and starts to uncover the body's face and neck. Vera gasps again.)*
VERA.   Oh!
MAY.   The bathroom's right outside. In the foyer.
VERA.   Bathroom?
MAY.   If you're going to be sick.
VERA.   Oh, no, I — *(Laughs, suddenly.)* I just — I thought it might be someone I know — *(May looks up from her work.)*
MAY.   Is it? *(Vera comes closer and for the first time, peers at the body's face.)*
VERA.   *(Relieved.)* No, no ... no one I know. *(May starts to wash the head with the cloth, wiping the eyes and nose gently.)*
MAY.   Soft skin, so soft ... like rice paper. Soft and silky.
VERA.   Should I — should I be saying any of this?
MAY.   *(Nodding.)* "Her cheeks are like a bed of spices,"
BOTH.   "Towers of sweet herbs.
Her lips are roses dripping flowing myrhh.
Her arms are golden cylinders — "
VERA.   "Her arms are golden cylinders set with beryl." *(Vera puts down the book and faces front.)* I've heard those words a lot of times since that night. But not like she said them. *(May covers up the face and uncovers the right arm. She begins washing it. Vera looks at the hand.)* What is that?
MAY.   Blood.
VERA.   I didn't know you could bleed after death.
MAY.   You can do a lot of things. You'd be surprised. *(May tenderly wipes each finger of the corpse's hand, as though washing the hand of a child. Vera speaks again to the audience.)*
VERA.   She did the whole thing that night. Cradled it in her arms like she was holding a baby. And all I could do was watch and say the prayers. And she never told, God bless her, what a simp I was. *(Sandy laughs, as May and Vera freeze in*

place.)
SANDY. She was a little different with me. *(Lights come up very dimly on Rise, D.C., with a scarf covering her hair. She and Sandy do not look at each other directly.)*
RISE. Oh, God.
SANDY. *(Calling.)* Where are you?
RISE. Upstairs.
SANDY. Let me see.
RISE. Just — put it back like it was, all right? Just put it back!
SANDY. I can't —
RISE. Please? I'll give you the answers in biology — I got an A on the test!
SANDY. I can't put it back! It has to grow out!
RISE. She's coming! She's coming up the walk.
SANDY. Just hold on, all right? I'll talk to her. Stay in your room!
RISE. She's going to kill me!
SANDY. Go! *(Rise exits. After a beat, May calls, "Rise?" and crosses to Sandy.)*
MAY. Why is my daughter's hair blonde?
SANDY. What?
MAY. Don't you "what" me. I saw you coming out of your mother's shop today —
SANDY. We were just —
MAY. She looks like a tramp!
SANDY. She does not! She looks nice!
MAY. What do you know about nice!
SANDY. More than you, snotty old witch. *(Pause. Sandy turns, facing the audience. May continues as before.)* That's not what I said.
MAY. *(Overlapping.)* I heard what you said. And if I thought —
SANDY. *(Overlapping.)* It's what I thought — It's just I ... I used to go by the houses on Woodview all the time, that's where they lived. And it seemed like the people must be so ... wonderful in there, you know? So it — I don't know, it bothered me she was so mad all the time. Every time I saw her she was mad.

MAY.   You think I'm stupid, you think I don't know —
SANDY.   What I said was —
MAY.   *(Overlapping.)* I know what you said. *(Sandy turns back to May.)*
SANDY.   I just think you're —
MAY.   I just got home from something, you know what it was? A washing, I washed a dead person, may she rest in peace. You know how old she was? Eighteen. Eighteen years old and she's in the car with her boyfriend and they're taking drugs and boom! All right? She's dead.
SANDY.   Was it — was it Linny Mayer?
MAY.   Was it — *(Pause.)* Yes. It was.
SANDY.   Oh.
MAY.   You were friends?
SANDY.   Ac — acquaintances.
MAY.   Acquaintances. When somebody dies they're never friends, just acquaintances.
SANDY.   But we were!
MAY.   What is it for, Sandy, so the boys will like you?
SANDY.   What is what for?
MAY.   The drugs.
SANDY.   It's —
MAY.   Because, you know, they like you when you stand up to them better.
SANDY.   I know that.
MAY.   Oh?
SANDY.   I stand up to them all the time.
MAY.   *(Smiles.)* I bet you do. What about Rise, does she stand up to them too?
SANDY.   Rise doesn't have a boyfriend, but if she did she'd stand up to him.
MAY.   You're sure of that?
SANDY.   I'm positive.
MAY.   Even with her hair done like a call girl?
SANDY.   She doesn't look like a call girl, Mrs. Davis, I promise she doesn't.
MAY.   No? What does she look like then?
SANDY.   My customers don't look cheap. And especially not

Rise. I made it look good.
MAY.   *(Amused.)* I see. So, why doesn't Rise have a boyfriend?
SANDY.   Oh she has lots of boy FRIENDS. But nobody she likes enough to go out with. You know how it is.
MAY.   You think I'm too strict? You think I'm being mean?
SANDY.   Yes.
MAY.   Tough. *(Sandy turns away from May again and faces front.)*
SANDY.   That's the way it was.
MAY.   Tough little cookie, aren't you? Like me.
SANDY.   She liked me. I could really feel she was like me.
BOTH.   Like me. *(Lights fade on this scene.)*

Scene 3

Lights up on Rise (minus the scarf) down center. She is sitting at a desk, wearing a white lab coat and talking on the phone. On the desk is an urn with ashes inside it.

RISE.   OK, you want the blood tested for T-cells and two U-samples for pregnancy. Um, I could have it for you by six. *(Brief pause.)* I can't — *(Sighs.)* I'll try for five thirty. All right? I'll try. Right. *(She bangs down the phone, angrily.)* You want it any faster I might as well pour it down the sink! *(Rise starts to get up, but is interrupted by May, who crosses to her desk. She stands behind Rise, out of her sight line.)*
MAY.   Hello, Rise.
RISE.   Listen, I'm really busy right now.
MAY.   *(Laughs.)* "Can I call you back?"
RISE.   What?
MAY.   Isn't that what you say when your mom calls?
RISE.   I don't know. I don't have a mom who calls.
MAY.   *(Sighs.)* It's a new year, Rise. It's new for everybody, even you.
RISE.   Okay, fine.

MAY. What's that on your desk, confetti?
RISE. You know what it is.
MAY. You are a really morbid person, you know that?
RISE. Oh leave me alone, all right?
MAY. You are alone.
RISE. I have a —
MAY. What?
RISE. Father, somewhere.
MAY. If I wasn't such a bitch?
RISE. A stubborn old bitch. That's what HE said.
MAY. Yeah? What else did he say?
RISE. You really want to hear?
MAY. Yeah, I do.
RISE. He said you spent your life in the funeral parlor —
MAY. I spent my life — listen to me Rise. Your zay-dee came out to live with us — remember? And I promised him, honey, because he made me promise, to give him a Jewish burial. But when the time came I had — pressure. And I gave in. So we spent thousands of dollars, Rise, on a fancy coffin, and flowers. And it was an abomination to him, but I gave in —
RISE. Because of the restaurant you mean? The customers —
MAY. But is it really such a big deal, Rise, who can have the best coffin? You know you can make a pine box for thirty-five dollars? You don't have to wear a thousand dollar suit. You can wear a plain white shroud and it's a good thing, Rise, it's a holy thing.
RISE. But then you —
MAY. Because I — what I didn't do for my father I wanted to do for somebody else. Can you understand that?
RISE. Yes. Yes, I can.
MAY. Why do you need this on your desk? Rise! It's a new year. Look. *(May crosses to Rise's desk and picks up the urn.)*
RISE. Don't! *(May steps back, holding the urn out of reach. She turns it over, spilling the ashes out.)*
MAY. Hey! Watch the ball come down in Times Square!
RISE. DON'T —
MAY. Out with the old year, in with the new!

RISE.   DON'T!! *(She grabs for the urn, which falls to the floor and breaks. May starts backing away, slowly. After a beat, Rise bends down to pick up some of the pieces.)*
MAY.   *(Gently.)* Rise —
RISE.   *(Upset.)* Sssh — sssh —
MAY.   Tell me, Rise. Are you —
RISE.   Wait —
MAY.   Feeling life yet?
RISE.   Go, damn you! GO!
MAY.   *(Shaking her head.)* Why, because he left that way? I don't want to.
RISE.   He won in the end, though, didn't he?
MAY.   Nobody won.
RISE.   You sat in the kitchen every night, watching TV —
MAY.   I thought he'd come back, I —
RISE.   And if I asked you to play you'd say —
MAY.   *(Laughing.)* Stop! Or I'll eat another chocolate pudding!
RISE.   Stop. Everything came to a stop. *(May faces front. Lights up on Vera, on the opposite side of the stage from May.)*
MAY.   I know it's against the Law, and I know in your eyes it's worse than having an autopsy, but the truth is I don't think I want anyone to see me like that, you see? I don't believe, you see, it's just not something I believe in anymore. So look, I'm — I'd like to be cremated. I've put it in my will.
VERA.   But you were the one who —
MAY.   Please, I know what I did. And frankly I don't think it matters what we do. We're all strangers anyway.
VERA.   You don't believe that.
MAY.   But I do. I know it's a terrible sin, but it's what I want. I didn't — I don't want him to find me again, buried under some stone in the town he grew up in. I waited for him long enough.
RISE.   All night, dressed in your traveling clothes, with your lipstick fading and the flowers on your hat going soft —
MAY.   I knew I'd have to be at work in a few hours. *(Vera crosses to a bench D.L. Sandy enters and joins her on the bench.)*

VERA. There were others, of course —
MAY. Listening to night sounds and trying not to sleep. *(May crosses to the bench. She picks up her hat, which is on the bench, puts it on, and sits between Sandy and Vera. Lights should be dim, like in a train station at night.)* I was tired, though, I was always tired.
RISE. Hoping no one would steal your purse or touch your thigh if you dozed off —
MAY. It was safer than it is now, but still, there was always a chance —
RISE. Thinking about him shipping off in a few weeks, lying in a field somewhere, in a foreign country, in the middle of all those bodies, with no one to bury him or say the prayers —
MAY. In the morning I'd go to the ladies room and wash my face —
RISE. You washed all their faces —
MAY. — and go to work —
RISE. All their faces and their hands, and the backs of their legs.
MAY. *(Remembering.)* Yes.
RISE. But you made damn sure no one would ever wash you.
MAY. No one wanted me.
RISE. I did!
MAY. Rise —
RISE. We told time by the TV shows. Six o'clock was Phil Silver. Seven was *I Love Lucy*. Then *What's My Line*.
MAY. Are you —
RISE. The early show. The late show. *Sid Ceasar and the Show of Shows*.
MAY. Are you feeling life yet?
RISE. *(Upset.)* NO! *(Rise stands up and crosses to the body. Sandy and Vera remain where they are, speaking to Rise from their seats.)*
SANDY. Rise? Are you all right?
RISE. You — you called me.
SANDY. No, you called —

34

RISE.   Never mind. I'm here.
SANDY.   You want to —
RISE.   Yes. I'm —
SANDY.   We're reading the prayers. Here.
MAY.   It's true the nights went slowly. But I never thought about death. *(In the following scene, May turns to Sandy or Vera from time to time. They do not respond to her, but continue to speak with Rise.)* But listen, I said. We're all here together. Why can't we make the best of it?
VERA.   "Her body is as polished ivory overlaid with sapphires."
SANDY.   "Her legs are pillars of marble set upon foundations of fine gold."
RISE.   "Her — her appearance is like Lebanon, as select as the cedars. Her mouth is most sweet and she is altogether precious. This is ..." *(Rise stops, suddenly. Vera and Sandy quickly resume the chant, and Rise joins in.)*
VERA and SANDY.   "This is my beloved —"
RISE.   "And this is my friend,"
VERA, SANDY and RISE.   "Daughters of Jerusalem." *(May turns to Vera.)*
MAY.   Me? I'm a Brooklyn girl. No, he's from out west. Midwest, actually. Chicago? Somewhere out there, I don't know. I'd like to stay here if we can. I've lived here all my life.
SANDY.   Rise?
RISE.   Yes?
SANDY.   We're going to have to lift her. Can you help?
RISE.   Oh. Yes. *(Rise turns the table on it's hinges. The top part of the table should now be standing upright.)*
MAY.   He comes with me to the station on Sunday nights. And we dance. Oh — the music they play on the — what do you call it? The loudspeaker. *(May gets up and begins to sway softly, as we hear recorded music: Something like "Dancing Cheek to Cheek"* by Irving Berlin. She moves joyously for a moment or two as the song is played, and then sings some of the lyrics.)*

---

* See Special Note on Songs and Recordings on copyright page.

Funny, when you like a song so much how you remember the words. Me? I'm not — oh, yes. It's called Bois de Rose. *(She lifts her wrist to Sandy's face, and then lowers it again.)* They give us free samples at the factory. For special occasions, you know? Like Mother's Day. Sometimes I snitch a little — only the small bottles though, I'd never take a big one! Some of them do, but I'd never do that. And I only took it once, really.

VERA. Careful. She's slipping.

MAY. You like it? I'm glad. I like it too. Hey, you wanna get something to eat? I mean it's late but — no? Well, listen, I've got a sandwich somewhere —

SANDY. Do you — do you want to do the ta-hah-ra?

RISE. What?

SANDY. Do you want to do the ta-hah-ra with us?

RISE. I — yes. Yes, I do. *(All this time Rise has been watching May. Slowly, she washes her hands three times, with the dipping cup.)*

MAY. I'm happy to share. I've even got some chocolate — don't tell anyone. The soldiers get it when they go out on G.D. Guard Duty! I'm sorry. I thought you knew that. *(She takes a bit of chocolate wrapped in paper from her sleeve and offers some to Vera. There is no response.)* Well, maybe another time. *(She sits, holding the chocolate in her lap. The music ends.)*

SANDY. And it is said, God is the reservoir of Israel.

VERA. And just as the reservoir of the ritual bath purifies the impure, so does the Holy One, blessed be He, purify Israel. *(Rise picks up one of the buckets and rests it on the table. Vera and Sandy get up and walk over to Rise. Vera picks up several pieces of the broken urn and brings them to the table. Then she and Sandy each take a bucket and stand near the corpse.)* Nine "kavim" —

SANDY. Twenty four quarts —

VERA. In buckets of eight quarts each —

SANDY. To be poured over the body when the washing is done.

VERA. And we say the words —

SANDY. Tah-hoh-ra hee. *(Sandy pours the bucket of water over the body. Vera pours out her bucket next. The water should come in a continuous stream, without stopping.)*

VERA. Tah-hoh-ra hee. *(Rise looks at Vera and Sandy, and then, slowly, pours out her water as they did.)*
RISE. Ta ... Tah-hoh-ra hee.
SANDY. She is pure.
VERA. She is pure.
RISE. She is pure. *(Sandy reaches under the table and pulls out several white cotton garments — pants with closed feet, a blouse, a robe, sash, apron, face cover and bonnet. Vera takes some of them from her. None of the clothes should have seams, bindings, or pockets. As the women dress the body, they tie the clothes loosely with slip knots.)*
VERA. Start with the pants and tie them around the waist. Aleph, Bet, Gimmel, Dahled ... four times. You see the shirt, Rise?
RISE. *(Examining the shirt.)* Yes.
VERA. No pockets, so you take nothing out.
MAY. My mother used to say, if you like chocolate, you'll —
RISE and MAY. Marry a dark man.
MAY. But he's not, I have to admit. Won't even tan laying out in the sun. *(Sandy and Vera have finished dressing the body and have been praying silently [reading in the book and moving their lips]. Vera takes a small bag of earth from the table and begins sprinkling it over the corpse.)*
VERA. The earth is from Israel. We just sprinkle it around.
SANDY. The eyes, heart, and the sex organs.
MAY. Well, does anyone mind if I have some of this?
VERA. And then the pottery, we put on the eyes, and over the mouth. *(Vera takes three pieces of the broken urn, and puts them over the eyes and mouth.)*
MAY. It's funny, you know? Here we are on the same bench, we came on the same train, we all have men in the Service.
VERA. We tie the knots to spell the name of God, see? Shah-die. *(Vera and Sandy twist a cotton sash around the waist of the body and tie it with three strips pointing towards the head, shaped to resemble the Hebrew letter "Shin.")*
RISE. Ma —
MAY. But we never talk to each other, do we? I mean re-

ally talk.
VERA and SANDY.   V'ale Sha Die Yee-Tane La Chem Ra-Chah-Meem.
RISE.   Please, ma — *(May turns to Rise.)*
MAY.   Just — Just take the big sheet and wrap it all around. All right? *(Sandy and Vera take a large sheet and hold it up. Rise walks in front of them, C.)*
RISE.   I — will.
MAY.   You cover her, and ask her to forgive you.
RISE.   Listen, ma —
MAY.   And you forgive her too. Right? Maybe.
RISE.   What you — what you said before, about cheating yourself?
MAY.   That's you. That isn't me.
RISE.   That lady in the picture hat.
MAY.   Which?
RISE.   Who waited all night in the station.
MAY.   What about her?
RISE.   I'm keeping her, ma.
MAY.   She died.
RISE.   She's alive, ma. I can feel her. Here. *(Rise touches her stomach.)*
MAY.   Yeah? Well you see how long she lasts. You just see how long she lasts.
RISE.   She'll be all right, ma.
MAY.   Oh yeah?
RISE.   I've washed her off. I've polished her like a jewel.
MAY.   Oh go on.
RISE.   You're not going to take her away from me.
MAY.   She's not —
RISE.   She is, ma. She's —
MAY.   What? WHAT?
RISE.   *(Slowly, realizing.)* She's here, ma. She's ... feeling life. *(Lights dim to blackout. End.)*

PROPERTY LIST 1: "FOREIGN BODIES"

2 pamphlets (VERA)
Purse with $5 bill (RISE)
Spray bottle of hairspray (SANDY)
Rawhide tie (bow) (SANDY)
Basin with water (SANDY)
Dipping cup (VERA)
Towel (RISE)
Telephone (RISE)
Hairbrush (RISE)
Cigarette (MAY)
Washcloth (VERA)
Bucket of water (VERA)
Comb (VERA)
Prayerbook (VERA)
Urn with ashes (MAY)
Big picture hat (MAY)
Chocolate wrapped in paper (MAY)
Pieces of broken urn (VERA)
Bucket of water (SANDY, RISE)
White cotton pants with closed feet (SANDY)
White cotton blouse (SANDY)
White cotton robe (SANDY)
White cotton apron (SANDY)
White cotton face cover (SANDY)
White cotton bonnet (SANDY)
Small bag of earth (VERA)

WHITE DAYS

(Part Two)

CHARACTER DESCRIPTIONS

SANDY, 33. Owner of a hair salon. Tough, funny, glamourous, complex, with a sense of play about her clothes; she is someone who enjoys fashion and knows how to use it to her best advantage. She is also vulnerable, and hungry for the mystical and spiritual in ways she may not even fully understand. Though her mother accuses her of being a "mystic," Sandy is nonplussed by this definition of herself — though others, looking at her, might consider her an unlikely mystic, if they considered her one at all.

EDDIE, 37, chef and co-owner of an Italian restaurant. He and Sandy have been married for two and a half years. He is passionate, warm, needy; and can never seem to get enough — sex, love, adoration — from his beautiful, independent minded wife. He has a sharp sense of humor and enjoys life — good food, good sex, good wine. Intimacy is important to him; he would like a family, children, and yet wants something more as well. For him, the answer comes more out of sensual rather than spiritual realms.

BETTY, 51, Sandy's mother and ex-owner of Sandy's salon. Betty is also elegant, fashionably dressed and coiffed; a businesswoman before it was accepted by society. She is tough and funny like her daughter; a feminist without ever having "tried" to be; but unlike her daughter, she is much more practically minded and sees religion more as a social avenue than a spiritual source; she would find more solace in a good hot bath than in prayers or rituals of any kind.

DEVI, 30, an observant Jew and attendant at the Mikveh (Jewish ritual bath). Self-possessed and gentle, she is a woman of strong ideals and quiet strength. She grew up in an orthodox home and Jewish observance is second nature to her. She both enjoys and respects it, and it is a source of comfort and direction in her life. She is married and the mother of three children, and is popular with friends and in her community. At the same time her life has settled into a regular, if sometimes hectic routine, and she is more affected by the passions of others than she knows.

DAVID, king of ancient Israel (to be played by actor playing Eddie). Sensuous, passionate, artistic. Ruler though he is, David himself is ruled by his own sexual desires in unexpected and dangerous ways.

ABOUT THE MIKVEH

The "Laws of Family Purity" — as they are called in Jewish Law, are a subject of great controversy among Jews. Most do not observe these laws, but there are Mikvehs — ritual baths — in nearly every Jewish community for those who wish to use them. The majority of people who go to the Mikveh are religiously observant.

The Mikveh is a body of water which, ideally, stems from a natural source such as a spring. In modern cities it is not usually possible to find this, so a Mikveh pool consists partially of city or county water and partly of collected rainwater. Though predominantly used by women, men immersed themselves before holidays or before studying Torah. Some observant men still use the Mikveh for this purpose today. However, the only legal obligation to go to the ritual bath is confined to women.

According to Torah law, it is forbidden for men and women to have intercourse when the woman is "niddah." The state of niddah (separate) includes the time of menstruation, for which one must count a minimum of five days, plus a "dormancy period" of seven days during which there is absolutely no bleeding. To count these seven days, a woman examines herself twice daily using a clean white cloth, to make sure there is no blood in the vagina. The days are counted from sundown to sundown. After the seventh consecutive day which is free of bleeding the woman goes to the Mikveh. There she immerses herself, says a prayer, and immerses herself two more times. Women also use the Mikveh after childbirth. After immersion a couple can resume their normal sex life.

Before going to the Mikveh, a woman is asked to bathe or shower thoroughly, as well as remove all makeup, jewelry, etc. Most Mikvehs employ a woman to make sure the users are properly prepared, and immerse themselves completely in the water.

WHITE DAYS

PROLOGUE

We are inside a building which houses a Mikveh, or ritual bath, in Ridgefield, Illinois, a southern suburb of Chicago. Time is the present. A scrim is stretched across the stage, and the lighting on it should suggest a pool of water. Some Hebrew lettering — part of the ritual prayers said on immersion — may be superimposed on a portion of the scrim. Sandy is standing downstage of it, wearing a long white bathrobe and holding a piece of white cloth in her hand. She is reacting to a man behind the scrim, whom we come to know as David. He wears a loose, flowing robe from the Biblical era. We should not be able to see his features, only his outline behind the scrim.

DAVID. Let me see it —
SANDY. What?
DAVID. The piece of cloth, hold it up —
SANDY. But —
DAVID. I want to smell it, wet against my face —
SANDY. Will you —
DAVID. All those days, I've thought of —
SANDY. Make me —
DAVID. Slowly —
SANDY. Make me do things —
DAVID. Yes —
SANDY. My beloved put in his hand by the hole of the door,
DAVID. And my heart was moved.
SANDY. I rose up, to open —
DAVID. To my beloved, and my hands dropped with myrhh,

SANDY. And my fingers with flowing myrrh —
DAVID. Let me see it —
SANDY. What —
DAVID. The white days are over. I want to see —
SANDY. I opened to my beloved —
DAVID. I want to see it now. *(Lights out on this scene. We hear pounding on an outside door. The pounding continues, and we hear Devi, calling in the dark.)*

Scene 1

DEVI. Wait! Sshh! Wait! I'm coming! I'll — Sshh! Baruch Hashem! I'll be right there. *(Lights up on Devi, who is dressed modestly and wears a head scarf.)* Come in! I'm sorry, the rain is — I can't hear you. What? Your daughter who's — I'm sorry, I can't tell you that. You know we have a separate entrance and exit so the women won't — when it's your time of month, you don't put an ad in the papers, right? Her husband is — if he doesn't know she's here why is he in the car? *(Sandy calls from off-stage.)*
SANDY. Devi!
DEVI. *(Calls, over her shoulder.)* Okay! *(Pause, turns front.)* No, no it's got nothing to do with unclean. Mrs. — what's your name? Look, Mrs. Fox, maybe you've never seen something like this — but — *(She squints, looking out into the street.)* Excuse me, can I help you? *(Devi blocks the doorway. Sandy calls again.)*
SANDY. Devi?
DEVI. Your wife is — I really can't let you in sir. They'll shoot me — the Mikveh fairy will shoot me. *(Laughs.)* I'm kidding. But I really can't let you in. I'll lose my job.
SANDY. Where are you?
DEVI. Please don't do that, please! I don't want to call the police, please! *(Devi holds out her arm and moves to close the door. Devi watches the man go, and then turns, slightly, addressing the "woman" she spoke to in the beginning.)* I know this must be

strange for you but I really can't keep her waiting anymore. Is he — well. I guess he's pretty upset right now. Well, look, maybe you can call me. All right? *(She takes a card out of her dress pocket and tries to hand it to the woman, but after a beat, she pockets it again.)* Why is he honking?
SANDY.   DEVI!!!!
DEVI.   *(Calling.)* Call me, okay? BYE! *(Devi looks out at the street. Eddie enters D.L. and calls out to Betty.)*
EDDIE.   Betty get in the car. Please? I'm — I'm very — this is very humiliating, I don't need — *(Lights up on Sandy, U. She is dressed in a white bathrobe. She has just taken a shower and a towel is wrapped around her head.)*
SANDY.   What's going on?
DEVI.   I'm sorry —
SANDY.   What was that noise?
DEVI.   Your mother's outside — at least she said she was —
SANDY.   My mother?
DEVI.   And your husband — he was wearing a leather jacket —
SANDY.   Did you see the car?
DEVI.   Um … white — a white Chevy —
SANDY.   That's her's. That's her car.
DEVI.   Did — did you tell him you were coming here today?
SANDY.   No!
DEVI.   So he didn't —
EDDIE.   A bladder infection. That's what she told me! I can't — I can't discuss my sex life with my mother-in-law!
SANDY.   I was going to tell him — I wanted to try it first. It's — you know — it's not that easy to turn around and say —
DEVI.   It's all right.
SANDY.   And he's —
DEVI.   You're not sure he'd understand —
SANDY.   He doesn't go very long — he doesn't like going very long without — you know.
DEVI.   It's all right. I understand.
SANDY.   Two or three days maybe, tops.

49

DEVI. You don't have to explain.
SANDY. Then he goes crazy.
DEVI. Crazy?
SANDY. Well, cranky. He gets really cranky. *(Lights up on Betty who enters D.R. She holds an umbrella, and crosses to Eddie.)*
BETTY. Look, I'm sorry —
EDDIE. Betty —
BETTY. I don't — I am not going to get in the middle of this —
EDDIE. I never said —
DEVI. Well how did they find you?
SANDY. I don't know. It's weird, isn't it?
BETTY. You were the one who called —
EDDIE. I was upset, I thought you might —
DEVI. Well do you still want to go on?
SANDY. What?
DEVI. Do you want to continue? We can stop if you like.
SANDY. *(Hesitating.)* Na — *(Pause.)* No.
DEVI. Are you sure?
SANDY. I — you know they all want a piece of me. And I always give in I — This is my time.
DEVI. All right then.
EDDIE. I thought she was — you know I thought she —
BETTY. I could have told you this was a —
EDDIE. How could you tell? It looks like a building.
BETTY. I knew it was a Mikveh.
EDDIE. Yeah? How?
DEVI. Well then — can you come here please? I need to see if there's anything — *(Sandy approaches Devi, and the women face each other. Devi begins to examine Sandy, turning her so her back is to the audience.)*
BETTY. I remember when I got married.
EDDIE. You're kidding!
BETTY. The rabbi's wife took me on a tour. They try to recommend it.
DEVI. Can you lift up your feet? That's right. *(Sandy lifts her feet and Devi examines them. Devi checks Sandy's toes, nails, hair,*

and eyes to be sure no dirt or hairs are present.)
EDDIE. Did you go?
BETTY. I took the tour. That's about all.
EDDIE. I don't believe this.
BETTY. Do you think she's getting frummie?
EDDIE. What the hell is frummie?
BETTY. Frum — orthodox! Like the women on the North side.
EDDIE. Oh, God.
DEVI. Nails trimmed, ooh, ve – ry short. Did you brush your teeth?
SANDY. Yes.
DEVI. Remove any and all jewelry, contact lenses, rings, earrings, dentures?
SANDY. *(Giggling.)* Absolutely.
DEVI. What?
SANDY. Dentures.
DEVI. I know but I have to ask. And you've, uh, gone to the bathroom?
SANDY. Three times.
DEVI. Open please. *(Sandy opens her robe, and Devi looks her over one last time.)* Okay. I have one more embarrassing question.
SANDY. Oh, boy, was my face red. *(Pause.)* You know, "Calling All Girls — Was My Face Red?" It was a magazine.
DEVI. *(Laughing.)* Calling all Girls, huh?
SANDY. Never mind. Ask me.
EDDIE. Look are you gonna just stand out there in the rain? Are you?
DEVI. Have you had intercourse since the start of your period?
SANDY. No.
DEVI. Great. You can go in.
BETTY. If she finds out you've been following her —
EDDIE. I saw her going in and out of there — I thought she was out with some — bozo.
BETTY. This is worse.

51

SANDY.   Can I — can I just ask you something?
DEVI.   Sure.
EDDIE.   Betty get in the car, all right? Would you get in the goddamn car? *(Lights out on this scene.)*

Scene 2

Lights up on Eddie and Betty. She is on one side of the stage, in Sandy's shop. Nearby is a barber's chair and a table with various beauty supplies. Betty is talking into a cordless phone and reading out loud from a Hebrew-English Bible. Eddie is on the other side of the stage, sitting at a table in a restaurant. He is speaking into a standard black telephone and leafing through another Jewish Bible. A stack of cookbooks is also on the table, which is set with a red-and-white checked tablecloth, candle, plates, champagne glasses, and silverware.

EDDIE.   Just tell me where it is. I can't find it —
BETTY.   Okay. Here — you ready?
EDDIE.   Na — what page?
BETTY.   Here. *(She reads.)* "When a woman has a discharge, her discharge being blood from her body, she shall remain IN HER IMPURITY seven days; whoever touches her shall be UNCLEAN until evening. Anything that she lies on during her impurity —" da, da, da … "shall be unclean. And if a man lies with her, her impurity is communicated to him —" wait! Where is it — okay, look. "When she becomes clean of her discharge she shall count off seven days and after that she shall be clean." Did you hear that? *(Pause.)* They call it white days — I guess because she's not bleeding anymore. And then she has to bathe in the Mikveh — EDWARD! Are you listening?
EDDIE.   *(Leafing through pages.)* I'm looking —
BETTY.   And by the way, I did not have this dogma in my house. I was a working woman, I always worked, and when she — she was in seventh grade and we went to the film —

there was a film about getting your period in school and we talked about it, I never in my life said one word that would make her think for a minute this was anything but the most natural — this is Leviticus, all right? There's no God in this. Leviticus was some ... GUY that hated women and his wife wouldn't sleep with him and he decided he couldn't deal with her when she was having her period.
EDDIE. Like you know.
BETTY. I do know! *(Eddie stops turning pages.)*
EDDIE. Seven days AFTER the period?
BETTY. The discharge.
EDDIE. What discharge?
BETTY. The period, Edward, that's what they call it in the Bible! *(Angry.)* YOU'RE NOT LISTENING —
EDDIE. I'm listening, seven days after the period, or the discharge, or whatever they call it, you —
BETTY. I call it a period. Sane people call it a period, sick people who think they're talking to God call it a discharge.
EDDIE. And these sick people say you can't have sex for seven days after the discharge —
BETTY. The period, Edward —
EDDIE. The PERIOD, for Christ's sake, Betty, what difference does it make —
BETTY. A LOT OF DIFFERENCE —
EDDIE. If you can't have sex —
BETTY. *(Interrupting.)* If you call it a discharge you're saying she's sick!
EDDIE. I thought you said it was —
BETTY. IT'S NOT, GODDAMN IT! *(Pause.)* It's not.
EDDIE. Stop yelling at me —
BETTY. Ssshh! Wait a minute —
EDDIE. I'm not going to — *(Sandy enters, stylishly dressed. Betty hides the book under the table.)*
BETTY. *(Whispering.)* Ssshh! Hang on! *(Betty puts down the phone. Eddie still talks into it.)*
EDDIE. And how do you know Leviticus? You haven't set foot inside a synagogue since she had her bat mitzvah. *(Pause. Sandy and Betty stare at each other. Eddie begins leafing through the*

book again.)
BETTY. You're late.
SANDY. Don't bust my knobs, Betty Ann. I'm —
BETTY. I've got five people waiting, you want to help me out here?
SANDY. Not until you tell me what you were doing today.
EDDIE. Some guy, I like that, Leviticus was some guy. *(Louder.)* What about the Hebrew translation, huh? Va-Yik-rah, God called. *(Pause.)* God calls, and you put Him on hold. *(He shifts in his chair, disgustedly.)*
SANDY. Outside the Mikveh?
BETTY. Oh.
SANDY. Don't give me oh.
BETTY. You don't have to talk to me like that!
SANDY. I'm just —
BETTY. I gave you this shop, which I start —
SANDY. You did not —
BETTY. WHICH I STARTED when you were in diapers —
SANDY. You did not give me this shop —
BETTY. If I didn't —
SANDY. And I still want to know what you were doing out there. *(Pause. Betty turns away and begins arranging things on the table.)* Well?
BETTY. *(Pause.)* Your husband thinks you're having an affair.
SANDY. What?
BETTY. He saw you going into the building — he was driving by and — *(Pause.)*
SANDY. Yeah?
BETTY. And he saw you and then he called me. I'm —
SANDY. Oh boy —
BETTY. I'm sorry —
SANDY. It's —
BETTY. It's none of my business. I know.
SANDY. You got that right.
BETTY. I said I was sorry —
SANDY. I know! I know. *(Pause.)* I'll talk to him.
BETTY. Good.

SANDY. It was kind of neat in there — well not *neat* but — well yes it was, it — it was really — clean, in there, I didn't expect it to be so — you know, like a spa. Except on the bathroom wall there's a checklist —
BETTY. Oh God —
EDDIE. *(Reading.)* Va – Yik – rah ... used to be called Toraht Ko-ha-nim — Laws of the Priests. English title, Leviticus, taken from the ... Septu — What? Septu-agint. Oh. *(Sarcastically.)* Great. Just go down to your local Septu-agint, pick up Leviticus. He's the one with the scarf ...
SANDY. Well they have to make sure you're really clean before you go in the pool — I mean bath. And the woman who checks you is —
BETTY. *(Appalled.) Checks you?*
SANDY. Well yeah —
BETTY. I don't — I really don't think I want to hear about this.
SANDY. But aren't you curious —
BETTY. That is one thing I would never be curious about.
SANDY. Oh, tough lady.
BETTY. I'm not a tough lady don't you talk that way to me. *(Pause.)* My youngest daughter gets married and pregnant —
SANDY. Why do I bother —
BETTY. Excuse me, did I say married and pregnant? I meant the other way around —
EDDIE. Hello? Hello? Ah, hell with it. *(Eddie hangs up the phone and exits.)*
SANDY. At least she got what she wanted —
BETTY. My oldest is a mystic —
SANDY. I'm not —
BETTY. You're mystical! Don't deny it!
SANDY. Don't you ever want to try something —
BETTY. Not like that —
SANDY. Don't you ever get sick of this place don't you ever feel —
BETTY. Of course —
SANDY. I mean sometimes I'm — I'm so ... full of it, I stink! Hair and makeup all day long —

BETTY. I know.
SANDY. Diets and gossip and other people's problems — it's — I need to get them off me. I forgot what I smell like, by now. I mean it's nice —
BETTY. All right —
SANDY. *(Overlapping.)* To know you're still there, don't you —
BETTY. Yes, but ... *(Pause.)* Can I just ask you something?
(Lights up on Devi, standing in front of the Mikveh.)
DEVI. Sure.
BETTY. Why this?
DEVI. This? Oh, THIS! Well ... let me see ...
BETTY. I mean it's such a strange thing — who would do it unless they were — I don't know —
DEVI. I guess I never thought about not doing it. I mean — my mother went —
BETTY. You're — look, you're a business woman, you own your own shop, come and go when you want —
DEVI. And it was a really special time for her — you know, getting away from the house, coming back all fresh and clean — she always looked so beautiful ... and then when I got married I saw what she meant —
BETTY. And this — it's like something my grandmother would do — she did, in fact — I know she did.
DEVI. Well — you need some time away, when you have children — I mean —
BETTY. Because she had no choice — you know in those days you did as you were told.
DEVI. Well if you — do you have any children?
BETTY. I mean I know you don't remember —
SANDY. No.
DEVI. Well anyway, when you come back it — well. Just doing all the preparation — the seven days when I check myself, each day I — I look forward to the time when I can be with him again, and then when I go to the Mikveh —
BETTY. But they were very strict about the Laws —
DEVI. I shower, wash my hair — like — you know, when you were getting ready for your first date? It's so — I like being able to have that every month. It makes the waiting

easier — well, for me it does..
BETTY. And neither she nor my grandfather ever touched in front of us. I guess — they couldn't if she was on her period — *(Laughs.)* And I don't think they wanted us to know when that was.
DEVI. I mean — the first part's not bad — I — I hope you won't mind my saying this — but I don't really like doing it when I have — I don't like doing anything when I'm — when it's that time of the month, it's — don't you find it messy?
SANDY. Well —
DEVI. But the week afterwards, that's — well that can be hard ... I just ... I guess I just like the way we do it. I never feel pressured —
SANDY. Right.
BETTY. But then when I grew up I knew I wasn't going to live like that, I — well all I ever wanted was to be a — you know, an American girl.
DEVI. It's just that — well, we have to measure our time, so — we can't really — we can't take each other for granted, you know? And I think sometimes if we didn't, well ... I'd hate to have the kind of marriage where one of us had to turn the other one down and then someone gets hurt ... I don't know ... you — you know what I mean. *(Lights out on Devi.)*
SANDY. Yeah.
BETTY. So now when I see these young people going back to the way it used to be I'm — I'm sorry, but after everything we've been through it's — what can I tell you? It's hard to believe. *(Pause.)* Are you listening to me?
SANDY. What?
BETTY. What, I'm pouring my heart out and she says what.
SANDY. You know, Betty Ann. Your hair's a mess.
BETTY. Yeah, yeah —
SANDY. Get in the chair.
BETTY. Just tell me ... are you becoming a frummie?
SANDY. A what?
BETTY. Like the women with the kerchiefs — you'll cut off

your hair and have children all the time?
SANDY.   Are you kidding? You're kidding, aren't you?
BETTY.   I just — *(Breaks off.)*
SANDY.   What?
BETTY.   You've got all these books lying around.
SANDY.   What books?
BETTY.   Prayers, Hebrew books —
SANDY.   Is that a crime?
BETTY.   Around the shop I don't —
SANDY.   They're not around the shop!
BETTY.   They're —
SANDY.   In my office. That's all. *(Pause.)* What?
BETTY.   Nothing. *(Pause.)* Don't cut it, all right?
SANDY.   How about your throat? Can I cut that?
BETTY.   No!
SANDY.   *(Laughs.)* Just get in the chair, ma — would you get in the chair. *(Lights out on Scene 2.)*

Scene 3

Lights up on Eddie in the restaurant. He is closing up, putting things away, when he hears knocking.

EDDIE.   Come on in. *(Pause. No one enters.)* Door's open! *(Still, no one enters. Puzzled, Eddie starts to move for the door when suddenly, Devi comes in, wearing a raincoat and holding her purse.)*
DEVI.   Excuse me.
EDDIE.   What?
DEVI.   I hope I'm not disturbing you.
EDDIE.   What are you doing —
DEVI.   Sandy told me you worked here.
EDDIE.   Yeah?
DEVI.   I — I felt very badly about what happened today.
EDDIE.   What happened?
DEVI.   You came to the door and I —
EDDIE.   Oh — oh, yeah. Well. I ... I usually don't — I

never did anything like that before. *(He clears his throat.)* Um ... excuse me, but isn't it kind of late for you to be out?
DEVI. *(Laughing.)* Why, do I look that young?
EDDIE. Uh, no. You really don't look young at all.
DEVI. *(Pause.)* Oh. Well — I didn't think so, I just — *(Pause.)*
EDDIE. What?
DEVI. *(Embarrassed.)* Well you looked so upset out there and I — I don't know, I didn't feel we really — I sort of shooed you away and I'm sorry. I wanted to tell you I was — I didn't mean to. *(Pause.)* Do that.
EDDIE. Look, I, uh ... I don't know your name —
DEVI. Devorah. My friends call me Devi.
EDDIE. Oh.
DEVI. Like Debbie with a V.
EDDIE. Yeah, okay, Devi —
DEVI. I just wanted to give you some stuff about the Mikveh so you'd understand a little more. Here. *(Devi reaches into her purse and pulls out some pamphlets. She gives them to Eddie, who puts them on the table.)*
EDDIE. *(Listlessly.)* Great. Thanks.
DEVI. You're welcome.
EDDIE. Is there going to be a test?
DEVI. *(Laughs.)* No, no, it's just for you.
EDDIE. Well, I'll look it over some time.
DEVI. *(Blushing.)* Well ... I'm, uh ... I'm sorry. Excuse me.
EDDIE. What?
DEVI. I — well. I just — *(Pause.)* I don't know why I came here I just — I don't know.
EDDIE. *(Smiles.)* That's all right.
DEVI. No it's not. I'm sure I've made things worse —
EDDIE. It's okay. It's no big deal.
DEVI. I just wanted you to know that ... I know these laws were given a long time ago. But I don't think we've ... outgrown them or anything. I still think they were meant for us.
EDDIE. Yeah, I can appreciate that.
DEVI. You can?
EDDIE. Yeah, it — well it doesn't have to mean that's how

I feel but —
DEVI. No no of course not I ... I just don't want you to think I'm.... I don't know. Working some spell on your wife!
EDDIE. That's ... I didn't think that ...
DEVI. I — she came by once —
EDDIE. Has she — how long has she known you?
DEVI. Not very long. She came by a few weeks ago and wanted to make an appointment. But that wasn't where we met, we met at the Nofzigers —
EDDIE. You mean that wedding?
DEVI. They're cousins —
EDDIE. That was ... that was that orthodox wedding. She did the wigs — *(Pause.)* I didn't know you were there.
DEVI. Well, that's where we met, and — *(Eddie picks up a pamphlet and begins looking through it, idly. Devi watches him, gets distracted, and then continues.)* Well. What — what kind of restaurant is this?
EDDIE. *(Reading.)* Italian.
DEVI. It's not kosher, is it?
EDDIE. *(Laughs.)* No. My partner wouldn't — there's no real market for it here.
DEVI. You'd be surprised.
EDDIE. Yeah, well, I guess I would.
DEVI. Well, anyway, I ... *(Pause.)* well I've never had anything like this happen before.
EDDIE. Like what?
DEVI. Someone comes in, and her husband doesn't know —
EDDIE. You know, that's something, isn't it?
DEVI. But I — I hope you won't be too angry with her. I have three children and it's ... it's really important for me to get away sometimes. You want to include everyone. But it's hard, you know, when you have a family, it's ... a lot. You have responsibilities. What I'm saying is, you're ... I think you're a special couple. You have ... not everyone has what you have. You seem ... well I know you care a lot about each other. But sometimes you have to be apart to ... sometimes you need apart time. If you think — *(Sandy enters, wearing a long coat and boots.)*

SANDY.   Hey, Eddie! *(She is about to take off her coat but stops as she sees Devi.)* What the — what the hell are you doing here?
DEVI.   Oh. I'm — I'm — sorry. I —
SANDY.   Did he — did he call you?
DEVI.   No —
SANDY.   Yes he did, why else would you?
EDDIE.   Sandy —
SANDY.   It's not enough you follow me all over town —
EDDIE.   I didn't —
SANDY.   You followed me, Eddie, I know you followed me!
DEVI.   It's really not his fault —
EDDIE.   OKAY! I'm guilty I followed you.
DEVI.   He really didn't call me.
EDDIE.   Because you won't talk to me I followed you, Sandy. And then she came to the door and told me to leave and I did. And that's all.
SANDY.   That's all, huh?
EDDIE.   No, that's not all. I was in here, I was getting ready to close and she came in with those — those.
SANDY.   What?
DEVI.   The pamphlets — I thought he might like to read them.
SANDY.   You didn't call?
EDDIE.   What, do you really think I'm gonna call her?
SANDY.   But why?
EDDIE.   But *I'd* like to know — I still don't know what you're doing —
SANDY.   Well if you'd give me a chance —
EDDIE.   Oh, right!
SANDY.   I was going to tell you.
EDDIE.   When, a year from now? You think I wouldn't notice, maybe, you weren't sleeping with me anymore?
SANDY.   Shut up, Eddie!
DEVI.   Please, can't we — *you*. You should sit down and talk about this —
EDDIE.   Yeah — sit down. Take off your coat. I have a lot of stuff I want to say right now.

SANDY. I can't.
EDDIE. What do you mean you can't?
SANDY. I can't take off my coat. *(Pause, as they look at her.)* There's ... I'm not — I can't take off my coat. *(Pause. Eddie and Devi realize Sandy is naked under her coat.)*
EDDIE. Really?
DEVI. *(Blushing.)* Oh my.
SANDY. Yes.
EDDIE. No kidding.
DEVI. Oh dear.
EDDIE. *(Pleased.)* I don't believe this.
SANDY. Yeah, well ...
DEVI. Uh, well, it — it was nice meeting you — *(Eddie answers but never takes his eyes off Sandy.)*
EDDIE. It was great!
DEVI. I'm — I'm really sorry.
EDDIE. I know —
DEVI. Goodbye.
EDDIE. Bye. *(Devi exits.)*
SANDY. I don't believe she did that.
EDDIE. Yeah, well —
SANDY. I mean what —
EDDIE. Maybe she was worried about you.
SANDY. I can take care of myself.
EDDIE. Absolutely.
SANDY. I mean it's my business if I want to — I wish you'd all just let me take care of my own stuff, you know?
EDDIE. Come here.
SANDY. What?
EDDIE. Take your coat off.
SANDY. I thought you were mad at me.
EDDIE. I am.
SANDY. Yeah?
EDDIE. Come here —
SANDY. How mad are you?
EDDIE. Come here I'll show you. *(He kisses her.)*
SANDY. You know Eddie —
EDDIE. Ssh — *(They kiss again.)*

SANDY.   I should've told you but —
EDDIE.   Open your mouth baby ... *open* your *mouth. (Sandy complies. Eddie kisses her more passionately.)* Come on woman, give it to me —
SANDY.   Eddie —
EDDIE.   What. *(Pause. Sandy pulls back a bit.)* Can't you give me thirty seconds — What's the matter? *(Pause.)* What! You want something to drink?
SANDY.   Okay.
EDDIE.   Some wine? You know it's not such a bad thing if your husband wants you. Most people would say you're — *(Lights up on Betty, in the salon. She leans on the chair and waves a comb in the air, making her point.)*
BETTY.   Lucky, I mean a man like that — I'm telling you you're lucky. *(Sandy grabs Eddie and kisses him, fiercely. Betty freezes in place.)*
EDDIE.   What are you —
SANDY.   Get some champagne, Eddie. Get the good champagne. *(Eddie leaves. Sandy wraps her coat around her, looking after him. Devi enters, U., dressed like she was in Scene One. She carries a white head scarf in her apron pocket. She is folding a towel, facing front. Sandy does not look at her.)*
DEVI.   Well it's nice — it's kind of nice he cares so much about you. And — you say you met him here in town?
SANDY.   I — *(Pause.)* yeah. I ... met him in the restaurant —
DEVI.   Really! *(Sandy turns and faces the audience.)*
SANDY.   I'd just bought the shop from my mother — I mean I finally finished paying for it — and we went in there to celebrate. *(Betty crosses to Sandy, and they embrace. They cross to the restaurant table and sit, as Devi watches them.)* And I couldn't eat the fish, I said, Oh God —
BETTY.   What?
SANDY.   I can't eat this. *(Eddie enters again, a napkin draped over his arm. Sandy beckons to him and he crosses to the table.)*
EDDIE.   What's wrong?
SANDY.   I don't know, it's — it smells.
EDDIE.   It stinks.
SANDY.   I wouldn't say —

EDDIE. No, no, I can smell it from here. I'm sorry.
SANDY. Malodorous fish.
EDDIE. What?
SANDY. Malodorous.
EDDIE. Is that, what, like ... melodious?
SANDY. *(Laughs.)* No. It's — my husband used to — my ex.
EDDIE. Your ex?
SANDY. Used to say things like that.
EDDIE. Well. It's good you divorced him then.
SANDY. Oh yeah.
EDDIE. Well. That's — malodorous. I'll have to remember that.
SANDY. Well, anyway —
EDDIE. Listen. I'm sorry about this. Let me give you something else.
SANDY. No, no, it's —
EDDIE. How 'bout lasagna? I make a great lasagna.
SANDY. I don't —
EDDIE. Three kinds of cheese, my own sauce, mozzarella —
BETTY. Take it —
SANDY. Ma!
BETTY. I'll finish whatever you don't eat. *(Eddie takes Sandy's plate, and exits.)*
DEVI. *(Laughing.)* Well, it's not easy to find a man who cooks!
SANDY. Oh he's amazing. He can make three kinds of pizza and they all taste different —
DEVI. Wow —
SANDY. But they're all really good and — you should see him tearing around the kitchen he's —
DEVI. I'm impressed.
SANDY. *(Sighs.)* He's a very ... passionate man.
DEVI. I can see that.
SANDY. And my mom adores him —
BETTY. He's real, he's a real person. Not like the first one, that professor. He was — what can I tell you? Not my cup of tea.

SANDY. So, anyway, we got married in the fall — September ninth —
DEVI. I was married in September! And it's funny we had to wait so long for the pictures —
SANDY. We didn't have any.
DEVI. Really, what happened!
SANDY. I mean by choice.
DEVI. You're kidding!
SANDY. Uh-uh. You know I really didn't want them. I mean it was a beautiful wedding — I wasn't ashamed of how I looked or anything — *(Eddie enters, carrying a new dinner plate.)*
DEVI. No of course not.
SANDY. We took the words from Solomon —
EDDIE. "Set me as a seal upon thy heart —"
SANDY. We even had them engraved on our rings. *(Eddie puts the dinner plate on the table and leaves.)* But I just didn't want anything to — well, like I told my mom — you have this incredible day and it's ruined by these trophies you stick out on the mantel. They're — I don't know, to me they're bad luck. I mean people come over and see this ... bride off the cover of Vogue and they look over at the real thing, and she's — she's got hips like a barn and thighs as wide as Montana. And there he is, of course the picture looks all right, in fact he looks like God in the picture. And then you turn around and he's losing his hair and his belly sticks out — and what if you fight, okay, there you are screaming and spitting at each other and you can't even do that alone. You've got this — you've got these witnesses. This — this dream couple. I don't want them staring at me. I don't want them poking their perfect little noses into my life.
DEVI. So did your mother — what did she say?
BETTY. It's just a memory —
SANDY. But it's not. People never look like their wedding pictures. They fix them — just like we do when we do their hair.
BETTY. Well I still think it's worth preserving — it's up to you but if it was me I'd want to remember something like

that. You did something special, you — *(Sighs.)* do what you want but I think you'll miss out.

SANDY.   She didn't fight me or anything. It's ... I don't know, I just think it's better if you don't — see it out there like that, you can still have it like you want, the image you have is something you choose ... it's — more of ... your own. *(The figure of David appears, behind the scrim. Sandy turns and crosses to him. Devi and Betty exit.)*

DAVID.   The days of waiting, the white days —
SANDY.   Are past —
DAVID.   And you —
SANDY.   Want —
DAVID.   Yes —
SANDY.   And you watch —
DAVID.   Thou art beautiful, O my love, as Tizrah, comely as Jerusalem.
SANDY.   Terrible as an army with banners.
DAVID.   Turn away thine eyes from me, for they have overcome me.
SANDY.   My beloved put in his hand by the hole of the door,
DAVID.   And my heart was moved —
SANDY.   I rose up to open to my beloved;
DAVID.   And my hands dropped with myrrh, and my fingers with flowing myrrh, Upon the handles of the bar.
SANDY.   I opened to my beloved —
DAVID.   But my beloved had turned away and was gone.
SANDY.   But my beloved turned away and — *(Lights out on David. Pause. Sandy puts her hand to her mouth, trying not to cry. Devi enters.)*

DEVI.   Well I like having something to look at because it makes me — I feel like I've accomplished something, I guess! You — you make a promise and — you commit yourself and — that's important. Of course you take a risk but — who knows? Maybe the picture won't be as good. Maybe you'll like real life better. You might be better friends than you were at first.

SANDY.   What?

DEVI. I said maybe you'll be better friends later on. Because you can't always do that in the beginning. You want too much. *(Eddie enters, holding a bottle of opened champagne.)*
EDDIE. This is nice, I think you'll like this. *(Devi exits. Eddie pours the champagne into the glasses on the table.)* You're really beautiful, you know that? *(Pause.)* Are you okay?
SANDY. Ye — I —
EDDIE. What's wrong?
SANDY. Nothing!
EDDIE. You know you can talk to me, Sandy. I'm not some guy, I'm not some asshole trying to put the make on you. *(Pause.)* Are you sure you're okay?
SANDY. Yes —
EDDIE. I mean you don't have cancer or something —
SANDY. Eddie!
EDDIE. Because you are really out there, you know that? I mean, I can't even find the outer stratosphere on this shit. I'm ... I feel like I'm on the moon. *(Pause.)* You want some of this? *(He indicates the champagne. Sandy shakes her head no.)* You want — *(Breaks off.)*
SANDY. What?
EDDIE. You ... want to take your coat off? *(Pause.)* No. You don't want.
SANDY. I don't know, I —
EDDIE. *(Overlapping.)* You want something else, maybe, a book, or a baby, or an island in the Black Sea —
SANDY. *(Overlapping.)* I came over here, and I was all excited —
EDDIE. And I just look at you, I look at you and I want —
SANDY. And then I got here and then — she's here and I don't know what she's doing and —
EDDIE. I want you to sit down like we used to at midnight when I closed the store and you'd be waiting for me at the table in the corner —
SANDY. I don't know, Eddie, it seems like somehow it just —
EDDIE. And I'd bring us some wine, in champagne glasses, and we'd sit down, across from each other — *(Sandy and Eddie sit down across from each other. Sandy begins to unbutton her*

coat. She holds it open, facing Eddie, though we do not see underneath.)
SANDY.   It slips away from me, maybe ... I let it slip away —
EDDIE.   And you'd take off your shirt, and smile at me, and dip — *(Eddie leans forward, expectantly. Sandy mimes dipping each breast in a glass of champagne.)*
SANDY.   When I — when I met you, it was a miracle, it filled me up —
EDDIE.   First one, then the other, inside the champagne glass ...
SANDY.   And then something happened, something happened and I didn't even know — it's ... like it happened in my sleep —
EDDIE.   Looking at me —
SANDY.   And it's weird because I want to want you — *(Eddie looks intently at Sandy.)*
EDDIE.   What?
SANDY.   Huh?
EDDIE.   You were saying something, what did you say?
SANDY.   I ... *(Pause.)* Nah. I wasn't saying anything. *(Sandy buttons her coat.)*
EDDIE.   You want some ... eggs?
SANDY.   Eggs?
EDDIE.   An omelet maybe? I've got some leftover pizza.
SANDY.   Yeah?
EDDIE.   I made it the way you like.
SANDY.   Um ...
EDDIE.   Thin with the crust on the ends.
SANDY.   Pizza. Yeah, well. Okay.
EDDIE.   San?
SANDY.   Yeah?
EDDIE.   Can I — can I just ask you something? *(Lights up on Devi, at the Mikveh. She holds a white head scarf.)*
DEVI.   Sure.
SANDY.   What?
DEVI.   It's just that — well, we have to measure our time — so we can't really — we can't take each other for granted, you know? And I think sometimes ...

EDDIE.   Never mind.
SANDY.   Wait —
EDDIE.   I have to warm up the pizza.
SANDY.   Eddie —
DEVI.   I'd hate to have the kind of marriage where one of us had to turn the other one down —
EDDIE.   WHAT!
SANDY.   I know I should've told you but —
DEVI.   And then someone gets hurt. I don't know. You — you know what I mean.
SANDY.   I just wanted to see what it was like and — and — then last night I was looking at some of those pamphlets — *(Sandy picks up the pamphlet from the table.)* And there's one — they talk about some of the people who used the Mikveh in the past. And one of the examples they have is the story of David and Bathsheba — King David, and this woman he saw.... Anyway I looked it up last night and read it — and this morning when I went over there — *(Sandy puts the pamphlet down and crosses to the beauty salon. She slips off her boots, takes a brush and starts brushing her hair.)*
DEVI.   Now take your time. Be sure to look at the checklist —
SANDY.   I thought about it again ... this — well — David was standing outside his palace and he saw a woman named Bathsheba —
DEVI.   A lot of women bathe AND shower — so feel free if you like —
SANDY.   She was married to someone else —
DEVI.   Cut your nails on both hands and feet —
SANDY.   A man named Uriah.
DEVI.   Well, anyway, you know what to do.
SANDY.   I just kept ... thinking about it.
DEVI.   I'll be outside, all right? Call me when you're done. *(Devi goes. As Sandy continues with this memory, she turns away from Eddie and should not look at him directly.)*
SANDY.   I mean ... I was sitting there, and I don't know, all of a sudden I could feel your eyes on me ... like you were watching me do this —

EDDIE/DAVID. From the roof he saw a woman bathing, and the woman was very beautiful to look upon.
SANDY. Like I was her, like I was ... Bathsheba. And — well, when he saw her — he found out she was married and he wrote a letter to one of his Captains — they were in a war —
EDDIE/DAVID. And David wrote in the letter, saying, set Uriah in the forefront of the hottest battle, and retire ye from him, that he may be smitten, and die.
SANDY. And then he sent messengers, and —
EDDIE/DAVID. She came unto him, and he lay with her —
SANDY. And the whole time — it just kept getting stronger, this feeling you were there — *(Pause. Sandy puts down the brush. She picks up a small white cloth from the table, and holds it up.)* And I — I started thinking about how you — how you move your finger, inside me — touching until I'm wet ... and I ... I took this piece of white cloth, I'd been doing this for seven days to make sure there was no blood —
EDDIE/DAVID. And when Uriah was dead he took her to his home —
SANDY. Blood running in the streets of the holy city —
EDDIE/DAVID. Red on the white Jerusalem stone —
SANDY. Because he wanted her ... so badly ... and I —
EDDIE/DAVID. Couldn't see, couldn't see anything else —
SANDY. I took the cloth and twirled it around ... like it was your finger, pressing and stroking inside me —
EDDIE/DAVID. Let me see it —
SANDY. And there, it's still white, seven days of white and it's over, the time of waiting is over.
EDDIE/DAVID. I'm impatient —
SANDY. But it makes me —
EDDIE/DAVID. I don't like to wait —
SANDY. Hungry, and you like it when I'm hungry —
EDDIE/DAVID. Yes.
SANDY. I like it too. *(Sandy puts down the cloth and stands. Devi enters.)*
DEVI. Now. When you go in, pull the cork on the wall and the rain water will come through — remember? We have to

have some water from a natural source —
SANDY. I know.
DEVI. And keep your fingers open and stretched, and don't close your eyes and mouth all the way.
EDDIE/DAVID. Between the flesh and the water only breath, her lover's breath while he watches her from the roof. *(Sandy turns and walks to the scrim at the back of the stage. She steps behind it, and we see her silhouetted in profile, approaching the ritual bath.)*
SANDY. The water is alive, and it smells like rain — *(Sandy takes off her coat. She steps into the "Mikveh.")*
DEVI. Down, that's right, all the way down ... good.
SANDY. I feel it licking me, lapping at the creases of my skin like a cat —
EDDIE/DAVID. I see her, she knows I'm there, and as she lifts her arm I can see her breasts —
SANDY. The breasts she gave to Solomon, her son, and she suckled him —
EDDIE/DAVID. And he woke us with the Song of Songs.
SANDY. Let him kiss me with the kisses of his mouth — *(Sandy bends her legs as if she is immersing herself in the water. Her hands are stretched outward, fingers apart.)*
EDDIE/DAVID. For thy love is better than wine.
   Thine ointments have a goodly fragrance,
   Thy name is as ointment poured forth;
SANDY. The king hath brought me into his chambers;
   We will be glad and rejoice in thee,
   We will find thy love more fragrant than wine.
(Sandy straightens her legs as if coming out of the water. She puts her hands down. Devi leans forward and holds out the white head scarf, as if she is about to put it on Sandy's head.)
DEVI. Wait. Okay, now.
SANDY. Baruch Ah-tah Adonai Elohenu, meh-lech
   Ha O-lum,
   Ah-share kid-shan-u B'mitz-vo-tav Vit-zee-va-nu
   Ahl Ha Tvee-lah.
DEVI. Blessed are You God, who has made us holy with

Your commandments and commanded us concerning immersion.
SANDY. Do I —
DEVI. Down again like before. *(Sandy bends once more, as if going down. Devi straightens up again, still holding the head scarf.)* That's right. *(Sandy stands up and takes a deep breath, as though she's been underwater.)* Again.
EDDIE/DAVID. Set me as a seal upon thy heart, as a seal upon thine arm,
SANDY. For love is as strong as death,
EDDIE/DAVID. Jealousy as cruel as the grave.
SANDY. The flashes thereof are flashes of fire,
EDDIE/DAVID. A very flame of the Lord. *(Sandy immerses herself once more.)*
DEVI. And when you're ready ...
EDDIE. Wait —
DEVI. Come up.
EDDIE. Sandy — *(Sandy straightens up and breathes again. Devi steps behind the scrim and holds the coat out, as Sandy goes behind it.)*
DEVI. Mazel Tov. *(Devi helps Sandy into her coat.)* May you go from strength to strength.
EDDIE. Wait. I don't — *(Sandy goes in front of the scrim. Devi exits.)*
SANDY. What?
EDDIE. You're — *(He breaks off. Sandy crosses to Eddie in the restaurant.)*
SANDY. WHAT?
EDDIE. You're trying to get me hot about something I don't want to be hot about.
SANDY. Eddie —
EDDIE. You are. It's working and you are.
SANDY. I'm just —
EDDIE. You're trying to get me to agree to something —
SANDY. I'm not —
EDDIE. Oh come on Sandy what are we talking about here?
SANDY. You talk about wanting me, but you don't know

how much *I* want — how much *I* wish — I saw that today in the water, Eddie. I just kept thinking if I could get somewhere deep, where no one was after me, if I could be still long enough to breathe, I could do it, I could find it, that ... part of me, like Bathsheba she's there but I can't get close. And I wish I could come to you Eddie. If you would let me come to you sometimes, even if it means you have to wait, there are worse things than waiting Eddie, a lot worse things. If you want me to be with you, really with you like I want to be then I've got to have some white days, Eddie. We've got to have ... a few, white days. *(Sandy and Eddie look at each other. She approaches him, and slowly they embrace as lights dim to blackout.)*

END

PROPERTY LIST 2: "WHITE DAYS"

Piece of white cloth (SANDY)
Business card (DEVI)
Umbrella (BETTY)
Cordless telephone (BETTY)
Hebrew-English bible (BETTY)
Standard black telephone (EDDIE)
Hebrew-English Bible (EDDIE)
Stack of cookbooks (BETTY)
Candles (BETTY)
Plates (BETTY)
Champagne glasses (BETTY)
Silverware (BETTY)
Purse with pamphlets (DEVI)
Comb (BETTY)
White head scarf (DEVI)
Towel (DEVI)
Cloth napkin (EDDIE)
Dinner plate with fish (EDDIE)
Dinner plate with lasagne (EDDIE)
Bottle of open champagne (EDDIE)
2 champagne glasses (EDDIE)
Hairbrush (SANDY)

SOUND EFFECTS

Water sounds

SHOOTING SOULS

(Part Three)

CHARACTER DESCRIPTIONS

DEVI, 35. In the past few years Devi's life has grown busier, and as she has more children and her husband works longer hours she has begun to feel overwhelmed. She still has strong ideals and a sense of humor; but she is plagued by a constant feeling of exhaustion and desperation, trying to live up to notions of perfection but frustrated that she is often falling short.

GERSHON, 37. Married to Devi. He did not grow up in an orthodox home but met Devi through a friend and was impressed with her depth and gentleness. They have been married since their mid-twenties; and Gershon at that time took on an observant lifestyle and has enjoyed it up to now. Lately money has been a problem and he is harried and exhausted, working several jobs and beginning to understand that things are not likely to change. Yet he is puzzled at the unhappiness he sees in his wife.

DR. NATALIE CARROLL, 39, gynecologist, African-American. She is bright, warm, funny, professional. She is just getting to know some of the women in the Orthodox Jewish community, and is not quite sure how she feels about them yet, or how (and if) they will accept her as well. She is married and has one child, and has recently made a private decision not to have more. However, she was raised in a big family and has had some conflict about this.

RABBI JOEL MESSINGER, 42, clergy for the local orthodox community. He is bright, gregarious, a "people" person. He has always wanted to be a Rabbi. He is also a workaholic; over-involved with his job and in some ways uses it as a kind of escape from family life. Yet he too is dissatisfied; though people are constantly asking him for answers, he realizes he cannot really help them, and it is a source of frustration to him. He is also a perfectionist, but hampered in this regard by his wife, who refuses to engage in perfectionism of any kind.

MALKA, 40, a reluctant "Rebbitzin" (Rabbi's wife). She met Joel when they were both in college; she was studying Jewish education and is actually a wonderful, energetic teacher although not currently employed. Malka is witty, perceptive and attractive. She dresses elegantly although her clothes are still in keeping with orthodox clothing styles, and she does not have the same kind of playful fashion sense as Sandy would. But she does enjoy looking good. She is sharply critical of others; and though her "observations" are often quite funny, they can often be quite sharp. For a long time, Malka has wanted to have a child but has not been able to and has begun to resign herself to that.

BETTY, 57, basically the same as in Part Two, a little more relaxed.

SHOOTING SOULS

Scene 1

We are in the town of Ridgefield, a southern suburb of Chicago. Downstage right is part of a bridge over the Calumet River. Spots of light or basins, filled with water in front of the bridge may be used to suggest the river. Two chairs are near the bridge. Stage left are twin beds inside the bedroom of Devorah and Gershon Newman. (This area also functions later as the Rabbi's study and as a doctor's examining room.) A closet, and two more chairs are nearby, toys and piles of laundry are near the bed. Gershon and Devi are asleep in one of the beds. Gershon wears rumpled trousers and T- shirt; Devi wears a nightgown or robe. We hear the sound of a shofar — a ram's horn blown on the Jewish High Holidays. As the shofar sounds, Rabbi Joel Messenger enters, downstage.

RABBI. Sleepers awake! *(Devi begins to wake.)*
DEVI. Gershon — *(Gershon groans and turns over in his sleep. The Rabbi crosses D.C. and faces the audience.)*
RABBI. Devorah … *(A baby's crying is heard in the dark.)*
GERSHON. Devi — *(The crying stops. Gershon rolls over and goes back to sleep.)*
RABBI. It's Tashlich, Devorah.
DEVI. It's —
RABBI. Tash – lich, to cast. *(He leans forward, still facing the audience, but speaks intently, as if he is giving a lecture to Devi.)*
RABBI. You must cast your sins —
DEVI. Yes, yes —
RABBI. And empty your pockets — *(The crying starts again, louder.)*
DEVI. I — I'll get some — wait — *(Devi sits up. She folds*

the baby blanket so that it looks as if there is an infant inside. The crying stops.)
RABBI.   It's the only time we have, at the start of the year. *(Devi stands, facing the audience.)* So if you should have regrets, if there are things you wish you'd done differently —
DEVI.   Yes —
RABBI.   Then remember the words of Micah:
DEVI.   Who is like a God unto thee, that pardoneth iniquity.
RABBI.   Mee Ail Cah – Mo – Ha No – Tay Av – ohn
DEVI.   And passeth by the transgression of the remnant of his heritage —
RABBI.   He retaineth not His anger for ever, Because He delighteth in mercy.
DEVI.   He will again have compassion upon us;
RABBI.   He will subdue our iniquities; And Thou wilt cast their sins —
DEVI.   Into the depths of the sea. *(With a rapid motion Devi flicks her arm, and the blanket unfurls. It is empty. Suddenly the baby cries again, sound off-stage. Gershon wakes. The Rabbi exits.)*
GERSHON.   Devi? *(Devi closes her eyes.)* What are you doing? *(Louder.)* DEVORAH! *(With a start, Devi opens her eyes. The crying grows louder, then soft again, stopping and starting intermittently under the following dialogue.)*
DEVI.   Gersh —
GERSHON.   The baby —
DEVI.   The ba —
GERSHON.   Is crying —
DEVI.   I *(Pause.)* I threw it —
GERSHON.   What?
DEVI.   It was Tashlich, and I —
GERSHON.   *(Annoyed.)* Never mind, I'll get him. *(Groaning, Gershon gets up and goes into the next room. The crying stops.)*
DEVI.   Threw my son — *(Pause.)* into the depths of ... the sea. *(Lights change. Devi exits. Dr. Natalie Carroll enters D.L., wearing a white lab coat. She is holding a portable phone against her ear.)*
NATALIE.   Where are you? What? I can't — where? Well it's a Jewish holiday. I know. But if — can't you come the

other way? On River Street. They're all at the bridge. I know the cars — what — what do you want me to do? *(Pause.)* Why don't you just give her a bottle I'll be home as soon as I can. I don't know. I'll take the bus. *(The Rabbi enters.)*
RABBI.   Malka! Did you bring the books? *(Malka enters.)*
MALKA.   What!
NATALIE.   You can give her a bottle, Jerry. Well she'll have to, I can't be there if I'm stuck, now, can I? *(Natalie peers out an imaginary window at the people on the bridge.)*
RABBI.   The prayer books —
MALKA.   Was I supposed to?
NATALIE.   It's — I'm not really sure. They're ... I think they're trying to throw their sins off the bridge. One of my patients — well how should I know?
RABBI.   All right, never mind. I told you to remind me.
NATALIE.   It's rush hour. I should be home soon.
RABBI.   It's my fault, I'm sorry, never mind. I have a sheet somewhere — *(Malka rolls her eyes. Rabbi rummages in his coat pocket and finds a pamphlet.)*
NATALIE.   Come on, Jericho. You can walk on water when you want to, I know you can take care of that baby 'til I get home. Don't — listen. Just put the banana in the food grinder — IN THE GRINDER.
RABBI.   Here. Ah ... Sam – Nu. Ba – Gad – Nu. Ga – Zal Nu ...
MALKA.   "We have trespassed, we have dealt treacherously."
RABBI.   Dee – Barn – Nu Doh – fee.
NATALIE.   Honey it's easy it's — *(Natalie waits, a beat, then slams down the phone.)* Great. And when you're done with the banana, do me a favor and put your nuts in there too. *(Natalie exits.)*
MALKA.   We have spoken slander — that isn't right.
RABBI.   What?
MALKA.   Well it's not Micah —
RABBI.   It's added, Malka, I added the reading this year.
MALKA.   Oh. Well, fine. What do I care.
RABBI.   Heh – eh – vee – Nu. F'heer – Sha – Nu.
MALKA.   We have acted perversely —

RABBI. And we have wrought wickedness.
MALKA. We sure have. *(Gershon enters and lies down in bed. Devi enters, with a baby carriage as we hear the soft mewling sounds of a baby's cry. She rocks the carriage, back and forth.)*
RABBI. On Rosh Ha Shanah it is written and on Yom Kippur it is sealed;
DEVI. It's all right, it's — Shhh ...
MALKA. How many shall pass away and how many shall be born;
DEVI. Sha, sha, sha, sha — *(The Rabbi sings.)*
RABBI. B'ROSH HA SHANAH TIK AH TAY VOON. OOH B'YOM TZOM KIPPUR, B'YOM ZOM KIPPUR TIK AH TAY MOON.
MALKA. Who shall live and who shall die; Who shall attain the measure of man's days and who shall not attain it. *(Devi is growing more frantic now, and rocks the carriage a little harder.)*
DEVI. Please God let him sleep —
RABBI. Who shall perish by fire and who by water —
DEVI. Let him sleep Baruch Hashem —
MALKA. Who by sword and who by beast, who by hunger and who by thirst.
DEVI. My hungry boy, my hungry —
RABBI. Who by earthquake and who by plague, who by strangling and who by stoning. *(Devi picks up the baby and sits on the corner of the bed, trying to nurse. The crying continues.)* Who shall have rest and who shall go wandering;
DEVI. Come on, come —
MALKA. Who shall be tranquil and who shall be disturbed;
DEVI. All right, then fine. Fine with me. *(She puts the baby back in the carriage, and listens, for a beat, as it cries. Rabbi's voice, in the meantime, has grown louder.)*
RABBI. Who shall be at ease and who shall be — *(Devi looks at Gershon, sleeping soundly. She tries shaking his arm.)*
DEVI. Gershon —
RABBI. Afflicted —
DEVI. Gershon I can't get him to eat and he won't stop crying —
RABBI. Who shall become poor and who shall wax rich —

(Devi turns back to the baby again. She is quite desperate now.)
DEVI.   Boychik what's the matter, what's the matter with you?
RABBI.   Who shall be brought low, and who shall be — exalted. *(The Rabbi exits, Malka turns to watch Devi and freezes in place. Devi leans over the carriage, and screams.)*
DEVI.   WHAT ARE YOU DOING — WHAT ARE YOU DOING TO ME? *(Gershon wakes.)* LEAVE ME ALONE —
GERSHON.   What —
DEVI.   LEAVE ME —
GERSHON.   DEVORAH! *(Devi turns, shaking, towards Gershon. The baby wails.)* WHAT'S THE MATTER WITH YOU! *(Pause. Gershon gets up and crosses to the carriage.)* What the hell is the matter with you.
DEVI.   *(Sobbing.)* Oh Gershon I'm sorry. I'm just so — *(Devi and Gershon embrace.)* Tired, Gershon. I'm ... *(Pause.)* just ... so ... tired. *(David and Gerson exit. Malka faces the audience.)*
MALKA.   If you can't say something nice ... I wish I could. I wish I could see something, someone, and not be so hateful ... I don't know. When I see people I never seem to see the good side. And I don't understand. How do I get so involved? He's involved. And he drags me in. He drags me into their lives. I wish he'd stop. I wish — *(Pause.)* I could tell him to stop. *(The Rabbi enters. He crosses to the bedroom, shifting the chairs to create his "study." Malka crosses to him.)* She's running amok.
RABBI.   Who, what do you mean, amok?
MALKA.   The rabbit queen —
RABBI.   Excuse me?
MALKA.   The perfect one. The one whose name we dare not speak ... she is so close to God.
RABBI.   What's that supposed to mean?
MALKA.   What do you think it means?
RABBI.   Don't get talmudic on me, Malka.
MALKA.   I'm not talmudic. I saw her outside of Toby's. I mean I was outside, she was in the restaurant.
RABBI.   Okay.
MALKA.   She was eating — Never mind.

RABBI.   What?
MALKA.   Nothing.
RABBI.   MALKA!
MALKA.   You know I don't like to talk about people.
RABBI.   You don't?
MALKA.   She was eating and — she had — *(Pause. Malka sits on the bed. Devi enters, holding a cafeteria tray with a plate, silverware and napkin on it. She is dressed modestly, and her hair should be covered. Gershon also enters and lies down on one of the beds. Devi crosses to the bridge, which now functions as a table in a restaurant. She sits. She uncovers the plate in front of her and pulls out a piece of food. She stares at it intently, and then, closing her eyes, crams several pieces into her mouth. Betty enters, walking through the room as though looking for someone. She spies Devi and squints at her, intently. Malka watches them.)*
BETTY.   Excuse me. You're ... *(Pause.)*
RABBI.   Maybe it wasn't her —
MALKA.   It was her —
BETTY.   — the Mikveh, aren't you? The woman at the Mikveh. *(Devi looks up and sees Betty.)*
DEVI.   I ... work there, yes.
RABBI.   You can't always see through a window.
MALKA.   I saw it was her. She was crying.
RABBI.   So maybe the food didn't agree —
MALKA.   It wouldn't. *(Betty approaches the table. Devi quickly covers her food with the napkin.)*
BETTY.   *(Smiling.)* I bet you don't remember me.
DEVI.   Well —
BETTY.   My daughter came to you. Sandy.
DEVI.   Oh, yes.
BETTY.   You look ... thin.
DEVI.   I'm — thanks.
BETTY.   Amazing — *(Betty edges closer to the table.)*
MALKA.   I'm not going to say anymore.
RABBI.   No?
MALKA.   Let her tell you herself. If she's so ... fine she'll tell you herself.
BETTY.   I can't believe I'd run into you — *(Betty sits. The*

Rabbi opens his book and begins to read.) Ohh. I can't — excuse me. I can't wear these heels anymore. Oh. My God. *(Betty takes off her shoes discreetly, under the table.)* I'm supposed to be meeting my accountant. I wanted Sandy to join us and of course —
DEVI. *(Interrupting.)* She's coming?
BETTY. Well I wouldn't count on it. But you never know. I haven't seen her myself lately. She's coming and going. She's going to school.
DEVI. I heard that, yes.
BETTY. Oh?
DEVI. Yes, what is she going for, again?
BETTY. What? Oh. Psychology. She's got a good basis for it I can tell you that. You want to be a shrink? Be a hairdresser —
DEVI. I can see that, yes.
BETTY. But I'm glad she's getting out of it, you know. And it's funny, I think — I think it might have started with you.
DEVI. What?
BETTY. Well she really enjoyed going to the Mikveh. I mean I think she still goes sometimes. Well. You would know better than I. *(Pause. Devi does not respond.)* Anyway. I had my reservations at first but if … well, if it's good for her then who am I to complain? Right?
DEVI. Right.
BETTY. So, you have a lot of people?
DEVI. What?
BETTY. Coming to see you there.
DEVI. Well I haven't been around much lately, I … have a new baby.
BETTY. Congratulations! How many is that!
DEVI. What?
BETTY. How many children do you have?
DEVI. Twenty eight.
BETTY. *(Pause.)* You must be very busy.
DEVI. In our little shoe.
BETTY. What?
DEVI. Never mind. Are you … a grandmother?

BETTY. I have two little boys in Ohio. Three and a half and six. They're beautiful boys, see? I'm very proud of them. *(She takes a picture from her purse and shows it to Devi, who smiles and nods.)* And Sandy's ... talking ... you know. But right now she's off here, she's there, and — *(Betty puts the pictures away and continues.)* I'll tell you, I'm not staying home with the kids. I've done my time, you know what I mean? I can't — you know, you want to go out, you want to see a movie — a movie? What am I talking about, a *meal* ... you get two seconds of turkey in your mouth and it's Grandma! Come here! But I'm talking away here and you're missing out on your lunch.
DEVI. Actually, I'm done.
BETTY. I hope I didn't bother you —
DEVI. No, no. I just — excuse me. *(The Rabbi looks at Malka.)*
RABBI. Come on, Malka.
MALKA. This is you, Joel. This is you all over.
RABBI. What's me?
MALKA. People do what they're going to do. You keep thinking you can save them —
RABBI. I don't —
MALKA. And you want me to do the same thing. *(Devi stands, facing Betty.)*
BETTY. Well I'll tell her I ran into you.
DEVI. And say hello.
MALKA. Hello, Devi.
RABBI. Devorah! Come in. *(Devi turns, and crosses to the study. Betty watches Devi go, then looks at her watch, briefly. After a beat, she exits.)*
DEVI. The door was open —
MALKA. Good. Can I get you some tea?
DEVI. No, thank you.
RABBI. I'd like some if you're — *(Pause. Malka glares at him but he persists.)* If you don't mind, Malka. Thank you.
MALKA. Devi? Would you?
DEVI. Thank you. But no. *(Malka exits.)*
RABBI. So, Devorah —

88

DEVI. I — *(Pause.)* I think I need to talk to you.
RABBI. Sit down. Please. *(Devi sits. The Rabbi looks intently at Devi, who is silent.)* Is everything all right?
DEVI. I'm ... expecting again.
RABBI. You are? My God, of course you are.
DEVI. What?
RABBI. I knew when you came in, there was something in the face, you can see it! B'sha – ah Tovah. You look beautiful. *(Pause. Devi does not respond.)* Let's see. The little one is what, six months?
DEVI. He will be soon.
RABBI. Is he sleeping through the night?
DEVI. *(Laughs.)* You're kidding.
RABBI. What would I know, I ... well. How's Gershon?
DEVI. He's at the store, he paints houses, he's a night watchman three times a week.
RABBI. You know it's amazing you two can find the time to — *(Devi looks at Joel, and he breaks off.)* Well, you have your hands full, I'm sure.
DEVI. Well, Yankel —
RABBI. Is he, what — three?
DEVI. He's five, and David is two and a half.
RABBI. And Ari —
DEVI. The older boys are in school.
RABBI. Five boys and they're all good. And a mother who never complains — *(Devi gets up.)*
DEVI. I should be going soon.
RABBI. Devi — Devorah.
DEVI. Yes.
RABBI. When are you due? *(Natalie enters U. She carries a patient's chart.)*
NATALIE. End of May, I think. Let's say the last week — I'd say the thirty-first.
DEVI. I saw the doctor today — *(Facing the audience, Natalie extends her hand and crosses D. Devi continues talking to Joel, as before.)*
NATALIE. Natalie Carroll. Hello.
DEVI. She took over for Dr. Feldman.

RABBI. She's — that's right. Schvatz?
DEVI. What?
RABBI. Malka says she was —
DEVI. Yes, Rabbi. She is. *(Pause.)* Does that upset you?
RABBI. No.
DEVI. Does it upset Malka?
RABBI. What? I have no idea.
NATALIE. And you're Mrs. —
DEVI. Devi.
NATALIE. And this would be your sixth?
DEVI. Uh huh. You ... say you took over for Dr. Feldman?
NATALIE. Yes. Is there a problem with that?
DEVI. What?
NATALIE. I know most of the women in your community have your own doctors —
DEVI. Oh, no, it's —
NATALIE. Mrs. Messinger left —
DEVI. You mean Malka?
NATALIE. She followed Dr. Feldman to Chicago.
DEVI. She would.
NATALIE. What?
DEVI. Never mind. You're a doctor, aren't you?
NATALIE. Actually I'm a plumber.
DEVI. That's funny. You look like a doctor to me.
NATALIE. Well, you know —
DEVI. Look, I'm sorry —
NATALIE. It's all right. It's nothing, I just —
DEVI. I don't need to see anyone else, Dr. Carroll. I'm fine.
NATALIE. Well. All right then. *(Natalie exits.)*
RABBI. So look, what did this doctor say?
DEVI. Nothing much. I had the children with me. And afterwards I dropped them off at home and Ari watched them so I could — I told him I had to go out.
RABBI. Out?
DEVI. To the restaurant.
RABBI. Okay.
DEVI. And — I don't know why I did this, I ... I had

some — *(Malka enters D.R., holding a cup of tea. She faces the audience. At the same time, Betty enters, lifts the napkin on Devi's plate and seeing bacon on it, reacts.)*
MALKA. Bacon.
BETTY. She was sitting there eating —
MALKA. — like it was her last meal.
RABBI. Devorah —
MALKA. I never saw anything like it in my life. I swear to God. *(Betty exits, taking the tray of food with her.)*
RABBI. What are you saying?
DEVORAH. Rabbi I'm sorry I — *(Pause.)*
RABBI. What's the matter?
DEVORAH. I just — I'm not sure if I'm ready for this —
RABBI. Oh, Devorah that's not true. Someone else, maybe. But you do things nobody else can do. I've seen you.
DEVI. But this time it's ... *(Pause.)* I don't think I can do it right now.
RABBI. So what ... are you asking me? *(Pause. Devi looks at the Rabbi, then at the floor, then back at the Rabbi again. The Rabbi stands.)* You know there's a story of a soul, it's from the time of the Temple in Jerusalem —
MALKA. Oh no.
RABBI. There's a child, you see, that's waiting to be born. And in this state —
MALKA and RABBI. The soul knows everything —
RABBI. Much more than she will ever know in life. And in this place, two angels are told to watch the soul, setting a light above her, and in this light she can see from one end of the world to the other. In fact she sees everything, much more than she ever will in life —
MALKA. Okay. I can either stand out here listening or I can barge in there and bring the tea.
RABBI. And in the morning one of the angels shows her the righteous in heaven and at night she is taken to hell.
MALKA. *(Sighing.)* I'll wait.
RABBI. And during the day the other angel carries the soul all over the world, and shows her where she will live and where she will die. And in the evening, he places her —

MALKA and RABBI. In the womb of her mother —
RABBI. Where she stays for nine months. And when the time comes for her to come out into the world, the angel appears, and tells her to go and the soul is sad, and says I do not want to go —
MALKA. I can't listen to this —
RABBI. And the angel replies, "Thou were formed against thy will, so now thou will be born against thy will and try always to return to the light where you belong." *(Malka crosses to the study, holding the tea. She brings the cup to Joel.)* And the angel pats the child on the mouth, and the light on her head goes out and at once the child forgets everything she learned, and comes into the world with a little crease — we have it — here. *(The Rabbi touches the crease above his lip.)*
DEVI. But ... if she's forgotten what she's learned —
RABBI. What I think it means, what *I* think is, we are always trying to return to the light — but we have to see both light and darkness in order to achieve that. And having children is the only way we can bring these souls to God.
MALKA. Thanks.
RABBI. I — what? *(Malka faces the Rabbi.)*
MALKA. Nothing. I'm interrupting, I don't mean to interrupt.
RABBI. And — well I don't believe He gives us more than we can handle — *(Pause. The Rabbi stops suddenly and looks at his wife, who is staring at him.)* Yes? *(Malka snatches Joel's tea, suddenly, and exits. Pause, he smiles weakly at Devi.)* Well. You say you — have you spoken to Gershon?
DEVI. I got home from the restaurant and he was in bed — *(Lights up on Gershon in bed. Devi crosses to him.)*
GERSHON. Sshh! Turn out the light.
DEVI. I have something to tell you, I have some news —
GERSHON. Ah ... Devorah. *(Gershon turns over on his back.)* I was dreaming. I dreamed you were an angel, washing me in the water like a child. I was grown, I was a man but you were bigger, and you held me in the water and rinsed my hair —
DEVI. It sounds lovely —

GERSHON. I have to go to work.
DEVI. It's Shabbos.
GERSHON. Then —
DEVI. We'll be eating soon —
GERSHON. No —
DEVI. Gershon —
GERSHON. I want to lie down again. I want to lie down in the water —
DEVI. Listen —
GERSHON. Leave me alone, Devorah. Please. *(He turns on his side and sleeps again. Devi turns back to the Rabbi. Lights out on Gershon.)*
DEVI. I look at him sleeping, the way he hugs the bed, like my little one does when he's sucking, and I think — this is the mother, the bed is the mother for Gershon and me. We suckle and sigh, and sleep in it's arms ... only Gershon is the one sleeping, and I'm sitting up, giving milk to my son. *(Pause.)*
RABBI. Devorah —
DEVI. What?
RABBI. I know you must be tired but —
DEVI. Well ... the truth is, Rabbi, there was — one more thing I wanted to tell you.
RABBI. Yes.
DEVI. I — you know when I stopped at that restaurant I had trafe.
RABBI. What?
DEVI. Some bacon. I know it was a sin —
RABBI. Devorah —
DEVI. It was ... good, though, Rabbi. I'm sorry to say it was ... awfully good. *(Lights change. Devi exits. Rabbi Messinger crosses to the bridge. He turns, facing front.)*
RABBI. Be charitable, and merciful, and save us, we are sorry ... I'm sorry ... I pretend that I know how to help them when I don't. I look at their eyes and I see what they hope for ... but I can't seem to help any one. If I tell them what God wants — it's ridiculous. I don't know what He wants. I listen, and listen, but I don't understand ... and

sometimes ... I don't want to listen at all. *(Gershon gets up and crosses to the Rabbi's study.)*
GERSHON.   Rabbi, I'm sorry. I know it's late.
RABBI.   But I know — one thing I always know — they will not stop coming to my door.
GERSHON.   I don't mean to bother you. *(Rabbi Messinger leaves the bridge and crosses to his study.)*
RABBI.   I know. *(Sighs.)* Come in, Gershon, come in. You look terrible.
GERSHON.   Thanks.
RABBI.   You look like a Marxist.
GERSHON.   There are no Marxists anymore.
RABBI.   You'd be surprised. What can I do for you? Sit.
GERSHON.   Well. My wife and I — she isn't feeling well.
RABBI.   She came to see me —
GERSHON.   She did? Then you know.
RABBI.   Mazel Tov. Sit! *(Gershon sits.)*
GERSHON.   I haven't been around much at home. I go to the store in the morning and three nights a week I'm working late. I get home at one or two and then Sundays I paint and do odd jobs. And Shabbos, I sleep. I don't go to shul anymore so I can sleep in the morning and give her a nap later on.
RABBI.   I've noticed you haven't been coming —
GERSHON.   The funny part is I drag myself into that store in the morning and make coffee and I'm sitting there with the irons and nails and dish racks and every conceivable kind of water pick and — you know there are people — there are people in this world that don't even know the difference between a nail and a screw. I mean I see them come in, a young couple, and they've just moved in, it's their first apartment. And she comes over with screws to hang the pictures and I'm looking, I'm looking at him and he doesn't know. So I show them the picture hooks, you know the little hooks you hang a picture with and they're so surprised she says "Ah! They're adorable!" It's like ... like I've given them a gift.
RABBI.   A hah.
GERSHON.   And then I ... well I come home and I mean

the minute I get there I'm, I don't know I want to turn right around and ... I lean over to kiss her and she's pale and pinched like a woman in a hospital, lines of pain around the nose. And I wish I could give her a ...
RABBI. What?
GERSHON. I don't know. A picture hook. A key chain that turns into a flashlight when you press it — a foot massage. You know they have this wonderful — if you have bunions you should see, it's a hydrobath you switch it on and the water swirls around even if you don't have bunions. I brought one home and —
RABBI. She didn't look so bad.
GERSHON. What?
RABBI. When I saw her —
GERSHON. She's exhausted. I mean we both are. I'm — my life has been reduced to a single goal.
RABBI. The nap. All the parents you talk to —
GERSHON. Well, so, count yourself lucky. *(Pause. Joel looks down at his hands. Gershon stands up.)* Rabbi I'm sorry —
RABBI. No, it's — just don't say that to Malka, it — she really wants —
GERSHON. Of course she does. I'm *(Clears his throat.)* I'm very sorry —
RABBI. *(Interrupts.)* Let's forget about it please.
GERSHON. All right I — sure. I just wanted to ask you —
RABBI. What, ask me what?
GERSHON. You know I never wanted to be a saint — what an idiot. A saint. I mean, I liked to think I could be ... a tzaddik. A righteous man. Not because I'm better than anyone else but I want to believe that someone is counting me, that what I do means something. Because my family wasn't, you know, religious, and when I married I wanted to — you know, she came from an orthodox family and I'm sure they looked down on me. Of course I never felt — she never made me feel I had anything to prove, but —
RABBI. Yes. I know.
GERSHON. So if other people ... fudge on the Laws, I don't want — I wanted to keep them, even if it means a

little sacrifice. *(The Rabbi stands, turning away from Gershon. He is angry but trying to control it.)*
RABBI.   It's not a sacrifice.
GERSHON.   What?
RABBI.   Having children is not a sacrifice. It's a gift.
GERSHON.   But if a couple has children, and they've tried for a long time to have a girl —
RABBI.   Look it's a mitzvah. If you can do it, you will. If you can't —
GERSHON.   But if the woman is unhappy —
RABBI.   Is it the *woman* who's unhappy?
GERSHON.   I don't know. Maybe I'm — maybe it's my fault —
RABBI.   Well this one came a bit soon, all right?... If you wait a few years, you'll both — you might feel differently.
GERSHON.   It's ... possible. I walked in the other night and she was cooking at the stove. And the baby was crying, in his crib, just fussing like they do. And I, well I was going to pick him up and she said No, Gershon. I don't want him to get used to being ... held.
RABBI.   Gershon —
GERSHON.   I'd better go, Rabbi.
RABBI.   I — *(Pause.)* if you need something —
GERSHON.   Yeah, well. You'll be the first one I call. *(Gershon exits. Devi enters with the baby carriage. She crosses to the bridge, facing front. The Rabbi exits also.)*
DEVI.   On the New Year it is written in the Book of Life ... who we are, and what will become of us. And on Yom Kippur the book is sealed for another year. And all we have, the only chance we have to make up for what we've done, is in the days in-between. And every year I've come to You and asked to be forgiven and start again. It made me feel so good, so fresh and clean ... like when I came home from the Mikveh and he was waiting for me. It was always like a wedding ... it's not a wedding anymore. *(Natalie enters and crosses to Devi's bedroom.)*
NATALIE.   It's about seven weeks. Mrs. Newman?
DEVI.   When she told me I just stopped it was — everything in me just ... froze.

NATALIE. Mrs. Newman.
DEVI. Yes, I heard you, I — one minute, I'll be right — excuse me, I just want to see — *(Devi parks the carriage, crosses U. and looks towards an imaginary waiting room. Calling out.)* Ari! I don't want him running all over the couch. It's your responsibility, Baruch isn't old enough yet. And don't let David drip his juice, all right? I'll be out soon. *(Devi turns, and crosses to the examining table.)*
NATALIE. Is he the oldest?
DEVI. What?
NATALIE. Your son —
DEVI. Oh, yes. It's not his fault but — well Baruch's eight and a half and I can't expect him to watch the little ones —
NATALIE. I know.
DEVI. Do you have children? *(The two women look at each other.)* I mean, it's none of my business I just — I was just curious —
NATALIE. I have a boy and a girl.
DEVI. That's lucky.
NATALIE. You think so?
DEVI. Well, I mean — for us it would be it's — well. In Jewish law, you're supposed to have at least one boy and one girl. In fact you can stop if — if that's what you have.
NATALIE. I see.
DEVI. Anyway. I know it sounds ... odd —
NATALIE. Not really —
DEVI. It's just that most Jews aren't having children so when people see us they say — *(Pause, she breaks off.)*
NATALIE. What? I bet I know.
DEVI. I bet you do. *(Natalie looks at Devi's chart.)*
NATALIE. Well. It ... says here you work at a —
DEVI. Mikveh.
NATALIE. *(Reading.)* It says ritual bath.
DEVI. Yes. I — we don't have sexual relations at the time of menstruation.
NATALIE. Okay.
DEVI. And then there's a waiting period ... anyway at the end of that time women go to the Mikveh to immerse them-

selves. Then they can be with their husbands again.
NATALIE. You know I think I heard something about this ... but do you like it?
DEVI. It's not a question of liking —
NATALIE. I mean your job?
DEVI. Oh, I — well it's not a job, really. But, yes, I like it very much.
NATALIE. Well that's something, isn't it? Not a lot of people can say that.
DEVI. Well I should be an example —
NATALIE. An example?
DEVI. To the others, to the women who come.
NATALIE. I'm afraid I don't —
DEVI. When they see me they should see I'm ...
NATALIE. Yes?
DEVI. That I follow all the Laws. And have, at least have a boy and a girl. I mean there are women who don't but ... I can't do that. I have to do what is right.
NATALIE. *(Pause.)* Ah hah. Well. *(Natalie looks again at the chart.)* Is there anything you want to ask me, any questions?
DEVI. No no, but ... do you think you'll have any more — do you mind my asking?
NATALIE. I don't know, really. I was kind of waiting to see — I want to give them attention, you know. I want to be there for them.
DEVI. Right.
NATALIE. And I can do it now, but I think with another ... I don't think I could do it, you know, and still be doing this.
DEVI. I could see it would be ... hard. I'm sorry. I didn't mean to intrude.
NATALIE. It's fine, don't worry about it. You, overall, you're feeling okay?
DEVI. Yes. I — *(Pause.)*
NATALIE. What?
DEVI. It's — nothing, really, I'm — I have a problem with — you know, the piles —
NATALIE. You mean — *(Pause.)* I gotcha. You have an in-

timate relationship with Preparation H.
DEVI. We go way back.
NATALIE. Well there are a couple of options we can talk about when you're, you know. When you're done.
DEVI. *(Sighs.)* I'm going to need the whole thing replaced. *(She puts her hands on her waist, and gestures downward. Natalie laughs.)* I know I shouldn't complain —
NATALIE. Why not?
DEVI. Well some people can't have any, and God only gives us what He knows we can handle.
NATALIE. Is that what God does.
DEVI. What?
NATALIE. I said is that ... what God does. *(Lights change. Devi takes the carriage and crosses to her bedroom. She parks the carriage and lies down on the bed. Natalie exits, as Malka and the Rabbi approach the bridge. Malka faces the audience until the Rabbi addresses her, then she answers him.)*
MALKA. I spend my life in the synagogue, watching people pray and eat herring all the time. I haven't seen a movie in years.
RABBI. You know why I added the reading —
MALKA. I don't want to know —
RABBI. Why can't I talk to you? Why is it so hard for you to let me talk? *(They turn away from each other and face front.)*
MALKA. Our Father, our king.
RABBI. Be gracious unto us —
MALKA. My husband is married —
RABBI. And answer us, for —
MALKA. To five hundred people —
RABBI. For we have created nothing.
MALKA. We have created nothing. That's true. *(Rabbi and Malka leave. Gershon enters, and takes the carriage to the bridge.)*
GERSHON. Sometimes I go to work when there's nothing to do. I say I have to fix something in someone else's house ... and I go to the river and sit, with coffee and a sandwich and a bench and the sky. And I know ... she's alone but it's so peaceful ... on the bridge — *(Gershon exits. Devi gets out of bed and begins to tidy up the room. She begins making the bed and*

nearly trips over some toys underneath. She reaches down and grabs them. She crosses to the closet, reaches up to put the toys away and as she opens the closet door a slew of toys falls out onto her and spills into the room. She cries out.)
DEVI.   DA-AH-AH! DAVID! COME HERE! *(She turns to see her son, off-stage.)* COME IN HERE AND TAKE THESE TOYS AWAY. NOW! DID YOU HEAR ME? WHAT ARE YOU DOING, COME *HERE. (Devi sits down in the doorway. She sighs.)* It's early, David. It's too early for this. I'm not going to chase you I — Mommy doesn't feel well. All right? *(She looks towards David again. She speaks more gently.)* Look. There's a little soul that's waiting to come down. It's living with Mommy and it shares all Mommy's food, just ... like you share. Only it's inside her belly, so it makes Mommy tired. And then I get mad ... when I shouldn't get mad. I know. *(We hear Malka's off-stage voice. Devi looks up.)*
MALKA.   *(Off-stage.)* Hello, David. Hanna's here. You know Hanna? You've seen her at Shul.... You know she's in the kitchen. She's making cereal for Yankel. You want some? Go ask Hanna to make you some, okay? *(Devi stands and watches Malka who enters, holding a cup of tea.)*
DEVI.   What are you doing?
MALKA.   I brought you some tea.
DEVI.   I hate tea.
MALKA.   Fine. I'll drink it myself. *(Malka crosses to the bed and sits, takes a sip of the tea, then recoils.)* I hate this stuff. Reminds me of being sick. You didn't have any coffee.
DEVI.   Yes I do. You don't know where to look.
MALKA.   Well excuse me.
DEVI.   I won't.
MALKA.   It was nice of me —
DEVI.   No it wasn't.
MALKA.   Well pardon me for living.
DEVI.   Go away.
MALKA.   I can't go away. Devi.
DEVI.   Don't call me that — *(Malka puts the tea down on a chair near the bed.)*
MALKA.   I'm sorry. Devorah. Hanna said —

DEVI. Why is —
MALKA. She's a good baby-sitter —
DEVI. I don't need a baby-sitter.
MALKA. She owes me a favor.
DEVI. Then let her clean your house. *(Devi turns away from Malka.)* If I want a baby-sitter I'll call up and ask.
MALKA. Okay, fine.
DEVI. What are you doing?
MALKA. I told you. I'm bringing you tea.
DEVI. You're snooping —
MALKA. I am not —
DEVI. Stop trying to be nice, Malka. You're not good at it.
MALKA. When I put my mind to it I can — besides I came here to ask you something.
DEVI. What?
MALKA. Can you — *(Pause.)* I need to go to the Mikveh today. *(Devi looks at Malka curiously.)*
DEVI. Is that why you brought Hanna?
MALKA. Well she could watch —
DEVI. Okay, give me half an hour —
MALKA. Take your time. I'm in no rush. *(Malka begins to make Gershon's bed.)* I don't know how you stay so thin, Devorah. *(Malka pulls out a pair of Gershon's boxer shorts from the bed. Devi takes them, quickly.)* I'm serious. You've had all those children and you look wonderful. It's not fair.
DEVI. Malka, go. I'll meet you at the Mikveh. *(Devi throws Gershon's shorts into the laundry pile.)*
MALKA. I can't —
DEVI. Did he give you an assignment today?
MALKA. Who?
DEVI. Who do you think?
MALKA. No, I — well I heard your news, of course. And I was thinking, you know — it's ... well, to help one person is Tee Kun Oh Lum. To repair the world —
DEVI. I know what Tee Kun Oh Lum means —
MALKA. And it's important that — well if we don't help each other, how can we expect God to be — I mean if we truly ... believe —

DEVI. Give it up, Malka.
MALKA. What?
DEVI. It's beyond you.
MALKA. Excuse me. *(Malka stands.)* I have done funerals, I have done shivva calls, I've gone to every bar mitzvah in this whole congregation. As much as he's done them I've done them too.
DEVI. All right —
MALKA. What I haven't done, what I don't know how to do, is play nursemaid to the queen for a day.
DEVI. Well thank you Malka. I'm so delighted you came, you've been so helpful —
MALKA. I suppose you think you could do better —
DEVI. I wouldn't think —
MALKA. Oh but you could Devorah I'm sure, you're so *good*, with your mitzvahs and your children and your —
DEVI. *(Laughs.)* Children! Oh, the children I can do. *(Malka gets up as if she had been slapped. She turns and begins walking out of the room.)* Where are you going?
MALKA. Home.
DEVI. I thought you said you wanted to go to the Mikveh.
MALKA. I don't think so.
DEVI. Wh — *(Malka turns back to Devi.)*
MALKA. The Mikveh doesn't work for women like me.
DEVI. That's ridiculous.
MALKA. It's true. I'm rotten to the core. I'm always criticizing people. I've no idea why. They all seem so — stupid to me. Stupid and wrong-headed. Gossiping and abusing themselves. And each other. I wish I could — forgive them more. I'd be a lot better off.
DEVI. Well the Rabbi seems to think you're all right.
MALKA. What does he know? Men aren't very discerning, you know? They're really only good for one thing. We should put them on stud farms —
DEVI. *(Laughs.)* MALKA!
MALKA. At least that way you know where they are. Right? You'd like that wouldn't you?
DEVI. You're sick —

MALKA. Pick one out when you need to —
DEVI. But go to the Mikveh first —
MALKA. Oh yes. You can't forget the Mikveh. *(Pause.)* Listen. I'll be downstairs —
DEVI. You know, Malka. I had no idea you could be this nice. *(Malka exits. Devi crosses to the bridge, faces front. Natalie enters.)* Adonai, forgive me. I've eaten — twice I've eaten forbidden foods, now. I guess You know about that.
NATALIE. Forbidden food?
DEVI. A cheeseburger. I broke the Laws of Kash-root. I broke the Laws forbidding us to mix our milk with meat.
NATALIE. I don't understand —
DEVI. I guess that means I'm like Eve, doesn't it. I've gone somewhere I shouldn't go.
NATALIE. You don't look well.
DEVI. It's like I'm fading ... and I can't.... I love my children, I'd do anything for them I tell them over and over again. When I was little my father used to tell us to look out the window for a shooting star ... we didn't see any but one day we did and came running to tell him. Abba, we said, and he said, look. When you see a star falling it means a soul is coming down to be born. And I thought — I felt so lucky to be a woman and have that neshama — that's the Hebrew word for soul. I used to imagine them shooting around in the sky like sparklers and the woman who had the most sparklers was the best ... the blessed one. And now I'm — I have all these children and — I snarl like an animal.... The other day I screamed at my little one so hard, I yelled as loud as I could in his ear I knew it was hurting him and he cried ... he was yelling for a cookie and I'd given him so many ... I want a girl if I could ... please ... have a girl, we could rest. I just wanted to rest. *(Pause.)*
NATALIE. I think — *(Pause.)*
DEVI. What?
NATALIE. Well, nothing, it's ... I'm not sure. You seem to be under a lot of pressure and it's none of my business but I think it must be awfully hard to be perfect all the time —

DEVI. You don't understand. These are Laws. You don't go against them without paying somehow.
NATALIE. All right but, I don't know, whoever's making the rules —
DEVI. Look, you don't believe, do you? *(Pause.)*
NATALIE. I used to —
DEVI. But not anymore.
NATALIE. Well I don't have Laws I follow but I do think it's here ... it's what we do for each other, not who we pray to. I don't know. I do think of God when I see the babies coming out and I reach — it's — inside it's water, and outside it's air, and I never know if they're going to do it until I — when they take that first breath it's like ... I always feel I'm taking it too. It's really ... something. It takes me a while to get back on the ground. So if there is some kind of judge, well ... it would have to be the children, don't you think? I just know it would have to be them. *(Pause. Devi looks intently at Natalie.)* But, anyway I was thinking, it's easy enough to find out if you want to know —
DEVI. I'm sorry, I really have to go.
NATALIE. You know we haven't — examined you, I haven't —
DEVI. My children are waiting. I don't — excuse me. I don't want to be late. *(Devi exits.)*
NATALIE. But I haven't seen you today — I haven't ... *(To herself.)* seen you ... at all. *(Natalie watches as the Rabbi enters, followed by Malka, and Gershon. They sing.)*
RABBI, MALKA and GERSHON.
 AH VEENU MAL KAY NU
 HA NAY NU VA AH NAY NU
 AH VEENU MAL KAY NU
 HA NAY NU VA AH NAY NU
 KEE AIN BANU MA AH SIM.
RABBI. For all these, Oh God of forgiveness,
 Forgive us, pardon us, and
 grant us atonement.
(Natalie picks up the phone and dials.)
NATALIE. Answer, please ... answer. *(Pause.)* Hello, it's — the machine.

RABBI.   Mee Ale Ka – Mo – Ka No Tay Ah – Vone
MALKA.   Who else but God would forgive — *(Devi enters, holding the baby who is wrapped in a blanket. Gershon greets her, and she smiles at him. He squints, as if he is seeing someone in the distance. Natalie puts down the phone and exits U.)*
GERSHON.   Who is that?
DEVI.   What?
GERSHON.   That woman over there — Oh. She went back in —
DEVI.   I don't see anyone.
GERSHON.   She went inside. *(Gershon looks at the baby.)* Do you mind if I hold him?
DEVI.   He's all right.
GERSHON.   Please?
DEVI.   I just don't want to wake him right now. *(Natalie enters, watching the others on the bridge. She is wearing a coat.)*
NATALIE.   You must be coming to get me. Comin' through all these Jews with that child in the back seat, screaming. What would you do if you had six, Jericho? What do you think we'd do?
RABBI.   And passes by the transgression of the remnant of His heritage.
GERSHON.   V' oh vay ayl Peshah Lish – ay rote Na Ha – Law – to
RABBI.   He retaineth not his anger —
GERSHON.   Devi.
DEVI.   What?
RABBI.   He will again have compassion upon us —
MALKA.   He will subdue our iniquities —
RABBI.   And you will cast your sins —
MALKA, GERSHON and RABBI.   Into the depths of the sea.
GERSHON.   Let me help you —
DEVI.   Well if —
RABBI.   For the sin we have committed before Thee under compulsion or of our own will.
DEVI.   Just ... be careful I'll — don't wake him up. *(Gershon holds out his arms and Devi slides the baby into them, slowly.)*

MALKA. And for the sin we have committed before Thee by hardening our hearts.
GERSHON. For the sin we have committed unknowingly, Devorah, I ask you to forgive me. *(Devi looks at him. Natalie goes off-stage.)*
RABBI. And for the sin we have committed before Thee with utterance of the lips,
MALKA. For the sin we have committed before Thee by sinful meditation of the heart —
RABBI. *(Sings.)*
    AH VEENU MAL KAY NU
    HA NAY NU V'AH AH NAY NU
    AH VEENU MAL KAY NU
    HA NAY NU V'AH AH NAY NU
    KEE AIN BANU MA'AH SIM
Malka would you ... sing with me. *(Malka joins him.)*
RABBI and MALKA.
    AH SAY EE MANU
    TZEDAKAH VA HESED
    AH SAY EE MANU
    TZEDAKAH VA HESED
    V'HOSHEE AY – NU.
RABBI. And now you may begin ... *(Malka, Gershon and Joel take white handkerchiefs from their pockets and empty them into the water below the bridge.)*
MALKA. I am sorry for my jealousy.
GERSHON. I am sorry I left her alone.
RABBI. I wanted children and I ... want them still.
MALKA. I wanted the synagogue to blow up.
RABBI. But there is such a thing as too much wanting, and this ... is what I did.
GERSHON. Aren't you going to throw your sins?
DEVI. In a minute, Gershon. You ... give me a minute alone, all right? I'll meet you at the house.
GERSHON. I can wait —
DEVI. It's nothing to wait for. I'll be there soon. *(Gershon exits. The Rabbi looks at Malka.)*
RABBI. Is she —

MALKA.   I'm taking care of it, go.
RABBI.   I thought —
MALKA.   Don't think, just go.
RABBI.   I … didn't mean to get you so involved.
MALKA.   You didn't? *(The Rabbi smiles.)* So. Can't I be involved if I want to?
RABBI.   Sure, but —
MALKA.   Happy New Year, Rabbi.
RABBI.   Happy New Year to you. *(The Rabbi exits. Devi sees Malka, who is staring at her.)*
DEVI.   What is it?
MALKA.   Don't look at me like that.
DEVI.   Like what?
MALKA.   Like I'm —
DEVI.   The enemy?
MALKA.   I'm not.
DEVI.   Neither am I.
MALKA.   You want to walk?
DEVI.   Walk?
MALKA.   Yeah, I don't know. Maybe stop and get a cheeseburger. *(Devi stares at Malka and then, slowly, smiles.)*
DEVI.   Who's buying? You?
MALKA.   I don't know. I can't spend money on Yontov.
DEVI.   Too bad. Neither can I.
MALKA.   Don't you want to get rid of them?
DEVI.   What.
MALKA.   Your sins.
DEVI.   *(Pause.)* I don't know.
MALKA.   You don't.
DEVI.   Well —
MALKA.   You know, you really are a case.
DEVI.   Look who's talking!
MALKA.   I may be a case but I don't want my sins — *(Natalie enters U.)*
NATALIE.   Sins!
DEVI.   Do you have so many?
MALKA.   I have a few.
NATALIE.   To think you get rid of them so easy.

MALKA. Sometimes ... I want what other people have. And I hate them for having.... I find all kinds of ways they don't deserve what they have. And I curse them —
NATALIE. Just by throwing them away.
DEVI. Is that so bad?
MALKA. Don't you think so?
DEVI. I don't know. I've done the same thing.
MALKA. Well look, Devi — I mean Devorah —
DEVI. You — you can say Devi to me.
MALKA. All right Devi I — you really are a good soul —
DEVI. You think so?
MALKA. Better than me.
NATALIE. And they have to go to the water —
MALKA. Well look, I'll leave you alone. *(Natalie exits. Malka has begun to turn away as Devi takes a handkerchief from her pocket. She begins scattering bread crumbs off the bridge.)*
DEVI. For scaring my children with anger, Malka. I won't do that again. *(Malka smiles and turns back. Devi faces front.)* For eating trafe ... for gossiping ... and ... *(Pause.)* for all the things I may have done. *(Pause. Devi has thrown all the crumbs away but one. This she holds in her handkerchief.)* And ... *(Devi looks at the handkerchief, closing her hand around it.)* This one I think ... I'll keep. *(Pause.)* This child will be the last one I have. And if it isn't a girl You — *(Pause.)* I hope You will forgive me ... but You may not. *(Pause.)*
MALKA. How will you know? *(Devi turns to Malka.)*
DEVI. My children will tell me.
MALKA. If you're forgiven.
DEVI. I think so, yes.
MALKA. But how —
DEVI. I think so, Malka. They'll find a way ... to let me know. *(Lights fade to black.)*

END OF PLAY

PROPERTY LIST 3: "SHOOTING S SOULS"

Baby blanket (DEVI)
Portable telephone (NATALIE)
Pamphlet (RABBI)
Baby carriage (DEVI)
Baby (DEVI)
Cafeteria tray with:
    plate of bacon
    silverware
    napkin (DEVI)
Book (RABBI)
Woman's high-heeled shoes (BETTY)
Purse with pictures (BETTY)
Medical chart (NATALIE)
Cup of tea (MALKA)
Toys (DEVI)
Boxer shorts
White handkerchiefs with breadcrumbs (MALKA,
    GERSHON, RABBI, DEVI)

SOUND EFFECTS

Shofar (a ram's horn blown on the Jewish high holidays)
A baby's crying
Soft mewing sounds of a baby's cry
Baby wailing

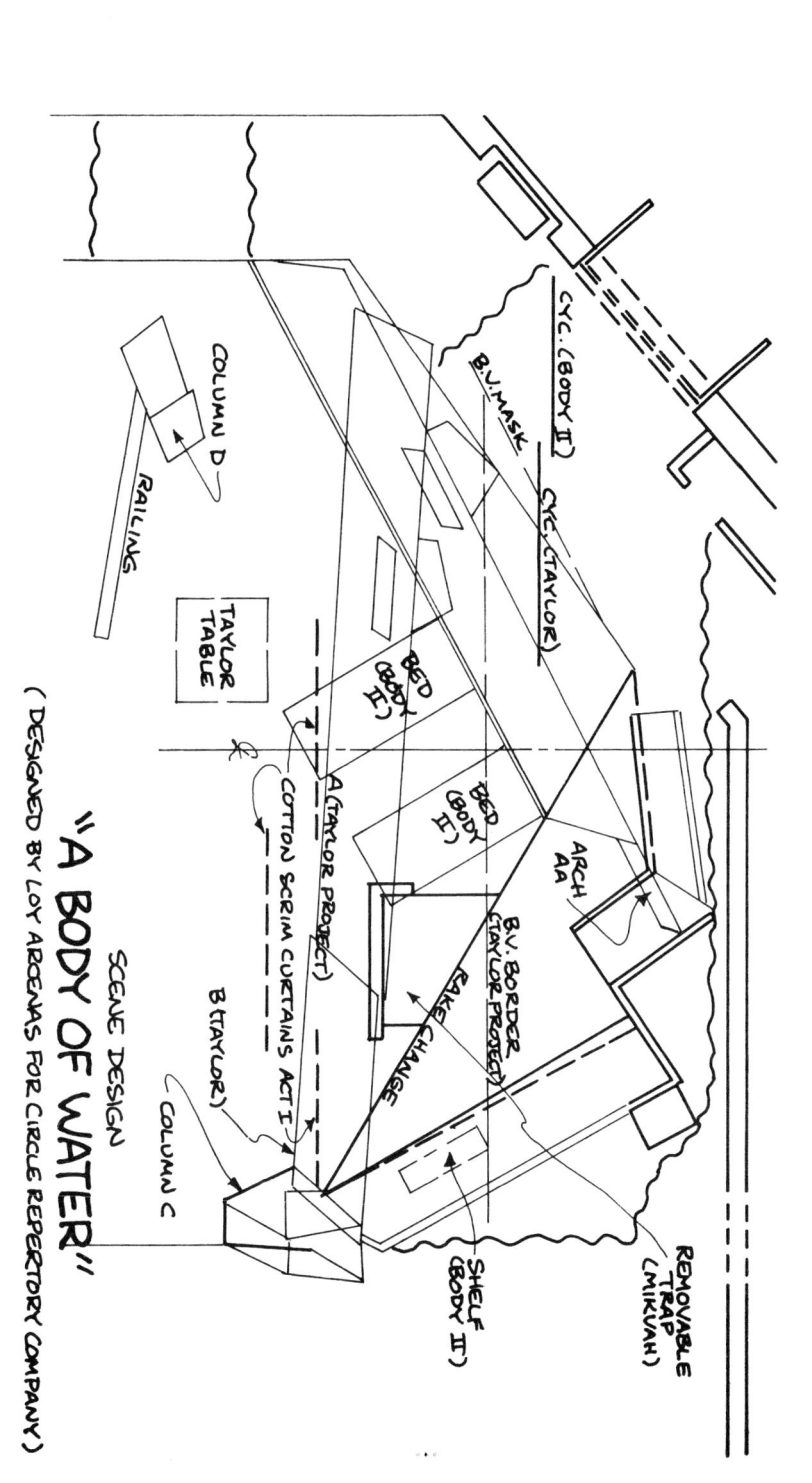

SCENE DESIGN
"A BODY OF WATER"
(DESIGNED BY LOY ARCENAS FOR CIRCLE REPERTORY COMPANY)

NEW PLAYS

THE AFRICAN COMPANY PRESENTS RICHARD III
by Carlyle Brown

EDWARD ALBEE'S FRAGMENTS and THE MARRIAGE PLAY

IMAGINARY LIFE
by Peter Parnell

MIXED EMOTIONS
by Richard Baer

THE SWAN
by Elizabeth Egloff

Write for information as to availability
DRAMATISTS PLAY SERVICE, Inc.
440 Park Avenue South   New York, N.Y. 10016

NEW PLAYS

THE LIGHTS
by Howard Korder

THE TRIUMPH OF LOVE
by James Magruder

LATER LIFE
by A.R. Gurney

THE LOMAN FAMILY PICNIC
by Donald Margulies

A PERFECT GANESH
by Terrence McNally

SPAIN
by Romulus Linney

Write for information as to availability
DRAMATISTS PLAY SERVICE, Inc.
440 Park Avenue South   New York, N.Y. 10016

NEW PLAYS

LONELY PLANET
by Steven Dietz

THE AMERICA PLAY
by Suzan-Lori Parks

THE FOURTH WALL
by A.R. Gurney

JULIE JOHNSON
by Wendy Hammond

FOUR DOGS AND A BONE
by John Patrick Shanley

DESDEMONA, A PLAY ABOUT A HANDKERCHIEF
by Paula Vogel

Write for information as to availability
DRAMATISTS PLAY SERVICE, Inc.
440 Park Avenue South   New York, N.Y. 10016